Red-Eye Coq
and 77 Other Delicious Things

ORIGINAL TWISTS ON FAMILIAR FOOD

Miles Morland
Illustrated by Hermione Skye

BY THE SAME AUTHOR

Cobra in the Bath

The Man Who Broke out of the Bank

To Georgie, who loved to cook
and who cooked with love

Two acknowledgements

I am to blame for everything in this book but there are two amazing women without whom Red-Eye Coq would be a sorry thing.

First is Hermione Skye. When contemplating doing a cookbook I looked in other cookbooks and saw that they were at least half glossy photographs. I then discovered that these photos were taken by professional photographers with lighting specialists, "food stylists", and other fluffers. I saw the need for this army of people when I tried taking my own photographs of food I had cooked. I'm not a bad photographer but, photographed by me, everything looked like gunge. Then, in a lightbulb moment, I thought of my honorary god-daughter, Hermione Skye, a brilliant artist who had done some murals for me. "Hermione, how would you like to do some food pics for my book?" "Oh OK, I'll give it a go…" And she did. The results are here for you to see. I suspect most of you bought this book because of Hermione's pictures, not my grey text in between. What pictures and what versatility. Thank you, Hermione.

Hermione will be making versions of some of the pictures in this book available as originals or prints. Or, if you are a person of taste, you may want to commission her to do a painting or mural for you.

Contact her at **hermione@hermioneskye.com**

My other thankee is Emma Charleston. I have written two previous books, both published by a big mainstream publisher. They are nice people but getting a book published by someone else takes the fun out of it. You have to do everything their way and fit in with their formulas and schedules. I decided to self-publish, not fully realising how much you then had to do yourself. I discovered Emma because a friend of mine had self-published a book which had the most brilliant layout including multiple photographs and illustrations. He introduced me to Emma, who had done it all. After that things became much easier. I handed the text and Hermione's pictures over to her. She put the book together and introduced me to Gemini, my printers. Without Emma I would have been lost. With Emma, I have a beautifully presented and laid out book of which I am more than proud. Thank you Emma.

If you are self-publishing a book, and, let's face it, who isn't these days, and you want to turn it from duckling to swan, get in touch with Emma.

Find her contact details at **emmacharleston.co.uk**

Miles has led an adventurous life.
He grew up in India, Iran, and Iraq, but has
his roots in England. He has motor-biked the
equivalent of twice round the world, across
the Andes and the Australian Nullarbor,
round Iceland, New Zealand, south India,
Japan, and Tasmania, through Death Valley
and across the Alps, Pyrenees, and Rockies.
Everywhere he has gone he has eaten the
local food and drunk the local drink. But the
more he has done that the more he has come
to recognise that in Europe we are lucky
because nowhere has better ingredients.
They are what Miles has come home to. And
what this book is about.

The Miles Morland Foundation

A few years ago I set up a foundation to encourage, enable, and empower world-class African writers: The Miles Morland Foundation. We have supported most of Africa's leading literary festivals, we have held writing workshops in Africa, and the annual Morland Writing Scholarships for African writers have become a feature of the African writing scene, attracting in 2020 almost a thousand submissions from published authors for four scholarships.

All profits from this book will go to the Foundation.

milesmorlandfoundation.com

A pre-COVID MMF Writing Workshop in Zanzibar

Contents

Man Learns to Cook

Like so many things, it started in New York. I was thirty-one; we had just moved there from London. Guislaine, my wife, who bore the burden of our move while I was busy shouting down a Wall Street telephone, had been born in New York and knew it better than I. She had been born there to Guy, a swashbuckling French father who had joined the US Army after the fall of France, and Gael, a glamorous half Irish, half Australian mother who had also been living in France when the Germans invaded and who had escaped into Spain by following goat tracks over the Pyrenees. Both were brilliant cooks.

So too was Guislaine.

We had moved to New York in 1974 away from an England that was close to breakdown at the time. New York was an exhilarating place in the 1970s but there was one big drawback compared with London. There were no Indian restaurants. Once a week in London we had gone to the Star of India in the Old Brompton Road, the Khyber in Bute Street, the Standard in Notting Hill, or any one of the many Indian restaurants for which London is famous, for a *dhansak* or a *rogan josh*. In 1974, New York had few Indians living there. Today, with changes in the visa laws, Indian restaurants are everywhere but then there

11

was not a Moti Mahal to be seen in Manhattan.

"New York was an exhilarating place in the 1970s but there was one big drawback compared with London. There were no Indian restaurants."

I missed Indian food. Knowing Guislaine's skill as a cook I gave her the *Penguin Book of Indian Cookery.* "Here, darling," I said, "perhaps you'd like to cook something from this. I'm really missing Indian food in New York." She riffled through the pages and handed the book back to me. "No thanks," she said. "Not my thing." I reminded her of the succulent *bhuna* prawns, delectably-spiced *brinjal bhajis*, and fragrant *biryanis* that we used to share in London. She was unmoved.

"If you're so keen on it why don't you give it a try."

Me? I could manage scrambled eggs and had at times fried bacon and burned sausages on the barbecue, but that was it. I had of course watched people cooking. My mother had been

an excellent no-nonsense cook, as she would have put it, and I had often stood hungrily in the kitchen while she turned out simple but delicious English food: roast chicken with bread sauce and scrunchy roast potatoes, veal and mushroom fricassée, cheese goo on toast, steak, kidney and Guinness pie, and the finest treacle tart in the world. But cooking looked complicated. I couldn't do that.

I reluctantly took the book which Guislaine had handed back to me with just the slightest of smirks and flicked through it. No dish had fewer than fifteen ingredients, each of which appeared to need complex and difficult treatment. Then I thought, hang on a second, half the world can cook, and this book is simply a book of instructions, just follow those and how difficult can it be?

I began flicking through the pages: *do piaza, gosht, bhuna, kofta, masala, sag, murgh*… I salivated as sauce-stained London menus sailed into my memory.

"OK. I'll do it."

"Wow," Guislaine looked startled.

"Just one thing."

"What?"

"Will you do the rice? I don't think I'd be up to that as well."

"Yes, of course. That's easy."

I decided that the coming

Saturday I would do a lamb *korma. Kormas* weren't too spicy so I would not have the added responsibility of having to get the chilli right. If I was going to do this I was going to do it the proper way. That meant finding whole spices and grinding them up myself; no ready-ground stuff in a bottle. The Yellow Pages and a short bus ride up Third Avenue took me to the All-India Food and Spice Emporium, one of the very few Indian shops in New York at that time.

"Then I thought, hang on a second, half the world can cook, and this book is simply a book of instructions, just follow those and how difficult can it be?"

I timidly showed my ingredient list to the owner. He gave it a two-second glance. "Ah, so it is a korma you are making?" "Well, yes. But it's my first time." "Don't worry, sir. We have only finest quality ingredients. All from India. You cannot go wrong." Easy for him to say. Soon things were piling up on the counter: ghee, coriander, cumin seeds, cardamom pods, sticks of cinnamon, cashews, poppy seeds, almonds, cloves… and then back downtown to our local food shop for lamb, yoghurt, fresh ginger, onions… this cooking was not easy work.

I began at 3.00 pm on a Saturday afternoon thinking it would take an hour, Guislaine and I could then go for a walk in the park and I would pop it back in the oven at 7.30 to warm it up for dinner. It took me five hours. Every spice needed to be ground by hand in a mortar but first half of them had to be de-podded. Have you ever de-podded cardamom? I hadn't. Even slicing and chopping onions is no easy business if you have never sliced an onion before. "Fry onions until translucent". Would that take one minute or half an hour? How hot? How were people meant to know these things? Thanks heavens for Guislaine who came over every few minutes to calm me down and answer my perplexed queries.

Then there was the matter of the *bhogar*. This, said the book, is an integral part of cooking *kormas*. When all is sliced, ground, browned and otherwise prepared you put it in a tight-lidded casserole which you set to simmer on the stove. From time to time you pick it up and give it a *bhogar*. This involves holding the lid on tight and

shaking the casserole sideways and downwards to stir up the ingredients inside. Easy. For people with three hands.

We sat down at eight to dinner, just the two of us. I was exhausted but the kitchen work had kept me so busy I hadn't had time to think of anything else. Tired maybe, but I was also strangely relaxed. The cooking had occupied my whole mind: no time to worry about work and bills. This was when I had my first insight into the wonder of cooking. It uses up just enough of the brain that you do not worry about other things but not enough of the brain to be taxing.

Guislaine took a sniff: "Mmm." She took a mouthful. I watched motionless. "Not bad. Not bad at all." I tasted it. Perhaps not up to Khyber standards but, for a first-time cook… not bad.

Seldom have I felt so proud. And that's how I started cooking more than forty years ago.

Since then my cooking career has been a random journey with many diversions. Once I had learned the basics I got fascinated by the complexities of *nouvelle cuisine* which was taking first France and then America by storm. I found myself spending hours deboning a sea bass completely, stuffing it with an exotic mixture of herbs, putting the

fish back together again so it looked untouched, and then making a complicated sauce reduced to a syrupy *jus*.

"The cooking had occupied my whole mind: no time to worry about work and bills. This was when I had my first insight into the wonder of cooking."

After a time I realised that the important thing was to let the ingredients, the raw materials, speak for themselves. Why smother a sparkling fresh fish or a leg of spring lamb with a complicated sauce or a crust of herbs? Few things today give me as much pleasure as cooking but the days of complicated sauces and reassembling deboned sea bass are long gone. I've tried to develop a simple style where the raw materials, pearly-fresh fish, farmyard chicken or spring lamb can sing for themselves while anything you add helps to bring out the taste, not cover it up. Herbs and spices are wonderful but they must never disguise the underlying flavour of the raw materials.

A Book for People who Want Second Helpings...

This is a book for people who love to eat. The test for the recipes here is simple. Do people ask for second or even third helpings? In this book you won't find recipes where people say "interesting…" but don't ask for a second helping.

Most of the recipes are ones that highlight the ingredients rather than the things that have been added to them.

We are lucky living in England, and I'm particularly lucky living on the Norfolk coast. Our gentle English weather with its mixture of sun and rain is ideal for growing so many fruits and vegetables.

Think how good our beans, peas, asparagus, lettuce, cabbages, sprouts, leeks, courgettes, onions and potatoes are. They may take longer to grow than they would in Italy or Spain but that gives them more flavour when they are ready to eat. Of course there are some things which do need sun. No English tomato is going to match an Italian one.

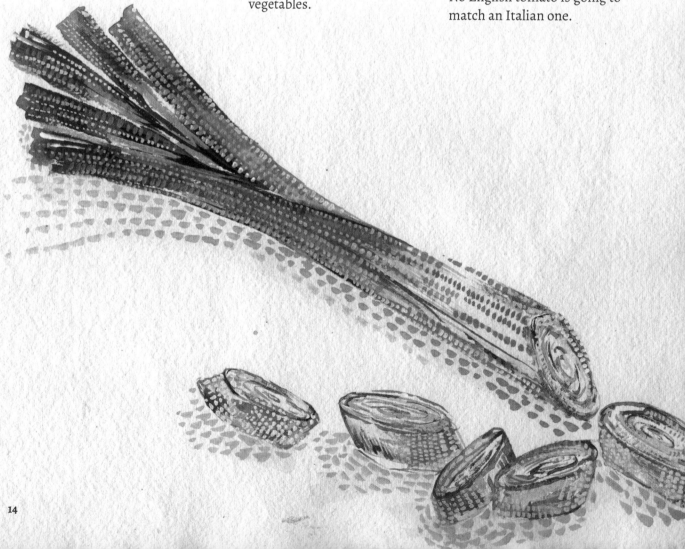

Our fish, meat and game are also among the best anywhere. Nowhere in the world produces better fish than the cold North Sea and the chilly English Channel. Why are the fish-loving Spanish so keen to fish in English waters? Our halibut, sole, turbot, brill, mackerel, cod, hake, and haddock are the best there is. Then there is English shellfish - cockles, oysters, lobsters, mussels, every kind of prawn and shrimp, and, my favourite because I live on the Norfolk coast, the brown crab, often called the Cromer crab. Compare a Cornish lobster with a Caribbean one… no contest.

I am lucky to have three old-fashioned Norfolk butchers, three independent green-grocers, three bakers, and two excellent fishmongers in Holt, my local town. All my butcher's meat has been reared in the open on farms within fifteen miles of his shop. He knows the first names of the farmers who produce it. In season his shop is full of game, not just pheasants and partridge, but also things like teal and woodcock which are absurdly expensive when bought in London but the price of a hamburger in his shop. In winter he even sells squirrel, a step too far for me. I suspect that because you are reading this book you have a similar local butcher close to you, one who cares about his meat and knows where it has been reared.

I would hope you can also find that much rarer thing, a good fishmonger. Supermarket fish has travelled a long way and been processed before it gets on the shelf. Avoid it if you can.

It would be a crime to mask ingredients of the quality the English countryside and coast can provide with elaborate sauces or herb crusts. The recipes in this book are ones where the cooking and preparation allow the quality of the ingredients to sing out. I would like to think that many of these recipes sound familiar but when you come to cook them you will find they have a special something you hadn't found before.

Some Tips on Food and Cooking

I assume that anyone who buys this book knows the basics of cooking. I'm sure you are also familiar with many wonderful recipes and your shelves are full of excellent cookbooks. I'm hoping you bought Red-Eye Coq in the hope it would inspire you to play around with the familiar. Toad in the Hole with no batter, pizza with no dough? Why not? Roast chicken submerged in milk curds? I have always loved eating. Below are some personal food thoughts.

1. Anchovies.

I have a small clip-top Kilner jar into which I decant the finest salted anchovies in olive oil I can find. It sits next to the cooking oil by the hob. Anchovies have a strong taste. Not everyone likes plopping a whole anchovy into their mouth, for me a wonderful appetite sharpener. Anchovies, though, are one of these ingredients which, used right, lose their own distinctive taste and make whatever they are added to taste richer and deeper. The Italians know this, which is why anchovies get pounded up and added to so many pasta sauces. The salty sharpness disappears while the sauce acquires a deep umami flavour. Very few stews and casseroles, particularly ones with red wine, are not improved by the addition of a few pounded-up anchovies. Put them in omelettes, scrambled eggs, and salads, and, if you are looking for a tea-time treat, squeeze some anchovy paste on to a piece of hot buttery toast.

2. Pancetta.

I buy slabs of pancetta, salt-cured pork belly, from a Spanish butcher who also stocks good Italian things. Pancetta is a slab of salt-cured Italian bacon. Because it is salt-cured you can eat it raw but its best use is sliced, chopped into lardons, and added to pasta, stews, casseroles, and often vegetables. When you buy your pancetta, it should be firm to the touch. If it's still squodgy it is too young and won't have developed depth of flavour. Find another supplier.

3. Cast-iron pans.

I cooked for many years on expensive Le Creuset "non-stick" pans. They annoyed me because, if you cooked at a high temperature, say for a stir-fry, you would end up getting hard-baked residue that was difficult to remove without harming the non-stick surface. In any case the non-stick surface wore off after a few years and you had to buy an expensive replacement. I can strongly recommend you go the cast-iron route. I won't explain in detail here because you can easily look their characteristics up online. My favourite is a 30 cm Lodge. It comes from America and is a classic. It is thick, dark, and extraordinarily heavy. It comes ready-seasoned so you don't need to go through the old-fashioned seasoning process. It is almost completely non-stick. You can cook at the highest temperature and it won't mind, although for most things, because of its ability to spread and retain heat, you can cook at a couple of notches lower than you would use for a normal non-stick pan. It is the best steak pan you will ever find. You do need to treat it right. Never use detergent or soap to wash it or put it in a dishwasher. If you do, you can destroy the non-stick quality and have to start again with seasoning it. Let it cool down, put some water in it, scrub with a soap-free scourer to remove any residue, let it dry, put in a drop of oil and rub that round with a paper towel. That's it. I also have a couple of smaller cast-iron pans which I use for omelettes, fried eggs, and things like that. If you have an induction or ceramic hob, do be careful not to drop your Lodge on to the surface. It's so heavy it would shatter it. Your Lodge will get better and better with age; you can pass it on to your grandchildren. You won't be doing that with Mr Le Creuset's non-stick frying pan.

4. Stock

…and stock cubes. No, nein, non… There are many better things you can cook with than a stock cube. Best is stock that you make yourself, not difficult. There are a few good (not many) bought stocks. Read the ingredients, the fewer and more natural the better. Wine is good. Even water is good and certainly better than a stock cube. People would be embarrassed to use these salt-bombs if it hadn't been for Marco Pierre White prancing around promoting them as the "basis of his cooking" for thirty years and heaven knows how many Knorr dollars. In order of importance, these are the ingredients of a Knorr chicken stock cube, starting with salt… (A Knorr chicken cube has more beef fat than chicken meat in it.) Salt, Sugar, Corn Starch, Monosodium Glutamate, Beef Fat, Hydrolyzed Corn Protein, Dried Chicken Meat, Autolyzed Yeast Extract, Chicken Fat, Water, Parsley, Disodium Inosinate, Citric Acid, Onion Powder, Partially Hydrogenated Soybean Oil, Whey, Sodium Caseinate, Natural Flavors, Colours (Yellow 5, Annatto, Yellow 6). Are you sure you want to add these nineteen ingredients to your casserole?

5. Bones.

Meat or fish, try to cook them both on the bone. Bones are where the flavour lies. It is the bones, not the meat that gives sauces depth. This applies to fish as much as to meat. A fillet of fish is a poor thing for flavour compared with fish on the bone.

6. Cabbage.

What a wonderful thing is cabbage. You can eat it raw in salads, chopped and briefly cooked with a squodge of butter or, my preferred way, shredded and stir-fried with a spoon or two of sherry or vermouth. A terrific soup addition.

7. Cheese.

What a sad world it would be without cheese. Fifty years ago English cheese consisted of cheddar, stilton and a couple more. Now my local Norfolk deli stocks thirty cheeses made in Norfolk alone. Cheese is so great in its own right, and has such a strong flavour, that I try to avoid the American habit of adding cheese to everything. This may be because American fast food is so bland that it needs something to give it taste. Who needs a tuna melt? I'm even reluctant to have a cheeseburger. Melted cheese is sublime while grilled meat and fish are equally good but mixing them deadens both. I love good Stilton, I love brie, some of our local cheeses are exceptional but for me two cheeses transcend the rest. Parmesan and Roquefort. Parmesan should be aged and eaten just by itself. Roquefort, so redolent of noble rot, is best mashed with a little butter, or scrumpled into a salad. Those two are my desert island cheeses.

8. Sausages.

Who doesn't like a sausage? The French, the Germans, the Italians, the Poles, the Spanish, and the Portuguese all make legendary sausages. They are so good that people tend to ignore the British banger. Ours is different to the continental sausages, which are usually dried and sometimes part cooked. The best British butcher's sausage is fresh and made from top quality pork with plenty of fat, a few simple herbs or spices, and a small amount of rusk or bread to give it texture. They are called bangers because in the days of rationing they had so much water added to them that they spluttered and spat unless you pricked them all over with a fork. Today you don't need to do that. Good ones have no added water. Sausages are often badly cooked. The worst thing you can do to a sausage is to put it on a barbecue. It's impossible to cook a sausage well on a barbecue. The best way to cook a sausage is to put it in a heavy frying pan with a little oil on a medium low heat and cook it slowly for 20 to 30 minutes by the end of which time the outside will be brown, caramelised, and a bit gooey. You can cook a sausage more quickly but it won't taste so good.

9. Ketjaap manis.

Sometimes kecap manis. What Worcester sauce is to English cooking, Ketjaap manis is to Indonesian. "Ketjaap manis is a thick, sweet, rich, syrupy Indonesian version of soy sauce containing sugar and spices. It's similar to soy sauce but sweeter. It's used in marinades, as a condiment, or as an ingredient in Indonesian cooking. The sweetness comes from palm sugar; other flavourings include garlic and star anise." I borrowed that definition from BBC Cooking. It is a key ingredient for me, used sparingly, in stir-fries and marinades. It's like a concentrated teriyaki sauce. Delicious. You can get it at good supermarkets and most places that sell Asian food.

10. Smoked haddock.

So good. So cheap. So simple. Scottish salmon is the king of smoked fish but smoked haddock and kippers are close behind. You can use them more or less interchangeably although haddock is much simpler to handle, prepare and eat than kippers. Both used to be sold yellowed with dye to show they had been smoked, Avoid dyed ones. They are invariably less succulent. Smoked haddock should be very pale in colour. It is wonderfully versatile. It has a great affinity with eggs. Poach it in hot milk for ten minutes and then flake the flesh off the skin; it will come away easily. The flakes themselves, served with a little butter and pepper, are delicious but better yet is to add them to an omelette, scrambled eggs, kedgeree, or a chowder. A *Smoked Haddock Chowder* recipe is in the book on p.61. Smoked haddock may be England's most underrated and best value fish. You can even slice it very thinly like smoked salmon and make a ceviche by squeezing lemon or lime juice over the slices along with tiny specks of finely diced tomato and onion.

Last, but it should be first measured by how often I use it and the results it gives, is...

11. Madeira.

The biggest importers of Madeira are the French. They never drink Madeira from a glass but use it all in their cooking, realizing what a brilliant ingredient it is. Many English cooks are obsessed with gravy. There are chapters on gravy in their books. They usually add flour to it, a great thing to do if you want your gravy to taste claggy. I try to avoid using flour in cooking. People often compliment me on the gravy I serve with meat, poultry, and game. I smile because I know how little work has gone into my gravy. I always have a bottle of medium-sweet Madeira to hand, Duke of Clarence is the easiest to find. Halfway through the roasting process I will pour a couple of glasses of this into the roasting tin around a chicken, say, or a leg of lamb. I add nothing else. By the end of cooking the Madeira has taken on the flavour of what is being cooked and absorbed its juices to make the most delicious gravy. Spoon it out into a jug and serve it with the meat. Try comparing that with the traditional English gravy made with flour added to it. You will be surprised at the result. The French know this. That's why they use so much Madeira. Join them.

Starters

My favourite starter at a dinner for eight or more people is charcuterie. Cover a couple of big wooden boards with mounds of sliced *iberico* ham, mortadella, thinly-sliced salami, radishes, maybe a slab of **Norfolk Country Pâté (see p. 28)**, and a bowl of cornichons. Serve that with country bread and butter. Not only does this taste good but people use their hands to eat, always a good way of making people unwind. As I say in the **Three Helpings Salad (see p. 32)** recipe, these days not everyone wants to start their meal with mounds of salted pig. It can be a bit much. If you don't want to take the pig route, I hope you'll find on the following pages some starters which are healthier and almost as good.

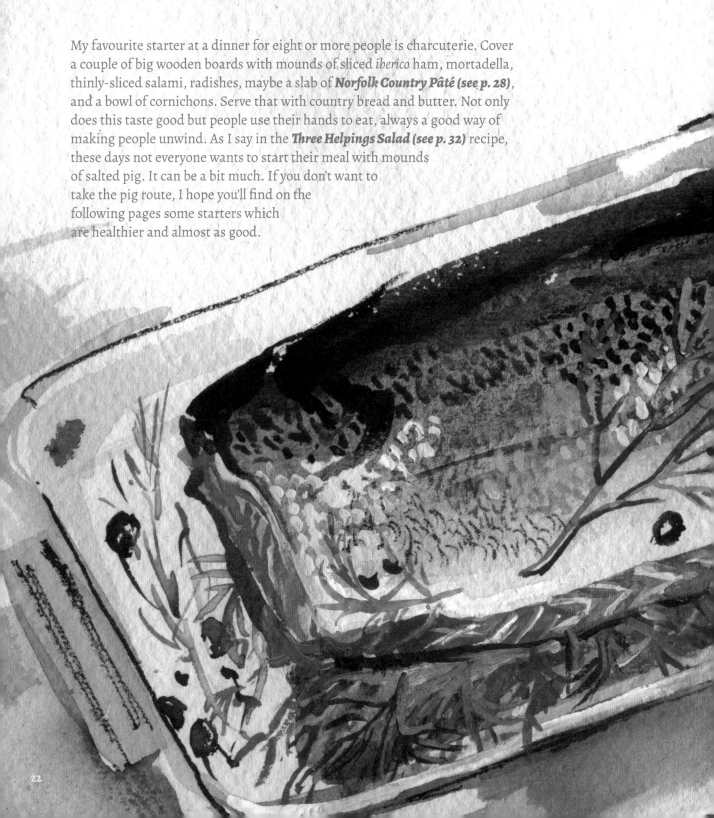

22

HOME-CURED VODKA GRAVLAX

How lucky we are that salmon is no longer a luxury. Top quality farmed salmon is pretty good. It's fattier than wild salmon but that's no bad thing if you're going to cure it. I have been making this gravlax for almost as long as I have been cooking. Smoking things is too much of a faff for me and home-smoked never tastes as good as shop-bought. Curing things on the other hand is a doddle and can taste far better than anything you will find in a shop. The last person who had my Home-Cured Vodka Gravlax said he thought it was the best thing he had ever eaten. Well, he was from New Zealand and he does have exceptional manners but I couldn't disagree strongly. It goes without saying that the fish must be really fresh and of good quality. This would not work with salmon you had bought in a supermarket.

Every recipe you see for gravlax will give you a companion recipe for mustard-dill sauce to go with it. "That's how the Scandinavians eat it," you will be told. Remember the Scandis are people who eat rotted shark meat. Do we need to follow them? I think not. Good gravlax has a great delicacy of flavour. Smearing it with a thick sludge of mustard, dill, cream, sometimes even horseradish and onion, would be like putting ketchup on sushi. Just a squeeze of lemon. Don't tell the Swedes but that is all you need.

The other area for debate is the salt-sugar ratio. That depends on your personal taste. I use the same amounts of both. If you want it sweeter, do more sugar and less salt, and vice versa for saltier. I find that equal quantities are just right.

> "Remember the Scandis are people who eat rotted shark meat. Do we need to follow them? I think not."

Ingredients for 8 to 10 as a starter

+ 2 salmon fillets (You can use a whole salmon but I wouldn't. The thin tail bit and the fat belly bit will cure at a different rate, giving you an over-cured tail and an under-cured middle. Get both sides of the whole middle bit of a biggish salmon, from the head back to where the salmon starts to narrow. They will weigh a kilo, maybe a bit more, and the fillets should be about the same thickness all the way along. Ask the fishmonger to remove the pin-bones, a fiddly job.)

+ 75g sea salt (I like Maldon)

+ 75g caster sugar

+ 1 tbsp black peppercorns

+ 1 tbsp juniper berries crushed

+ 80g dill, chopped but not shredded

+ 100ml vodka

What you do

Put the juniper berries and peppercorns into a mortar, crush them and mix in a bowl with the sugar and salt. Pour in the vodka and mix again. You will need a big plate, preferably an oval serving plate. Lay the fillets out skin side down. Massage the mortar mixture into the salmon, spreading it equally over both pieces. Spread the dill over one of the fillets. Take the other fillet and put it on top, skin side out, so both fillets are matching. Get a plate or board and put it on top of the salmon. Push it down to flatten the salmon and place something heavy on top of it. I use a cast-iron oval saucepan lid. Put it in the fridge. Take it out every 12 hours, take the top fillet off and lay it skin-down on the plate. The mixture will have created quite a bit of liquid. Spoon this over both fillets and then place the fillet that was on the bottom on top. Replace board and weights and back in the fridge. After three days, turning every 12 hours, take the salmon out and scrape off most of the mixture and dill.

Get a very sharp knife and carve vertically (not horizontally like smoked salmon) at a slight angle to give you slices the thickness of a piece of bacon. They should be thin enough to be almost translucent.

Serve with lemon quarters and either brown bread or toasted sourdough fingers.

This freezes brilliantly if you can't eat it all in one go.

MAGIC MUSHROOMS

Mushrooms are magic; it's that unique woodland taste. Essence of umami. Fresh mushrooms are good but it is the umami-rich dried ones that brighten up my winter. There are dozens of different types of dried mushrooms. On one hand are the Asian ones like Cloud Ears, Oyster, and Shiitake. I'm sure they're wonderful but I've never bonded with these. They can be slimy. In Europe, we revere porcini (aka cepe), chanterelles (aka girolles), and finest of all, the amazing morel. For me, two stand out, chanterelles and morels. I know that people rave about porcini. Rave on, because again I find they, like the Asian mushrooms, can be slimy although they do have a fine scent. The only trouble is that dried chanterelles are expensive and dried morels are beyond expensive. The good news is that, like their cousin the truffle, their taste is so strong that you don't need much of them.

If you are looking for a perfect cook-ahead winter starter, try this.

Ingredients for four

+ 2 handful of dried morels (less or none if you're feeling poor)

+ 2 handful of dried chanterelles

+ 10 golfball-size fresh button mushrooms, stalks off, sliced

+ 1 large onion, sliced

+ 4 rashers of streaky bacon, sliced into batons

+ 100ml rich Madeira (I use Duke of Clarence)

+ Splodge of double cream

+ 4 circular slices of toasted sourdough bread, crusts off

What you do

Soak the dried mushrooms for ten minutes in a bowl with 500ml of hot water. While they are soaking, sauté the onion and bacon in a large frying-pan over medium heat till the onions are soft and sweet. Take the dried mushrooms out of the bowl and squeeze their excess liquid back into the bowl. Put them on a board and chop roughly. Don't throw out the water they have soaked in. This is the best stock ever.

Add the dried mushrooms and the fresh mushrooms to the frying pan. Pour in half the stock from soaking the mushrooms (keep the rest till you next make a risotto) and the Madeira. Turn the heat up high and reduce the liquid while stirring with a wooden spatula. When the liquid has bubbled down to a syrupy consistency, you are done. It may take a few minutes. Add a small splodge of cream. By all means keep these hot for an hour or two in a covered bowl in the warm drawer.

When ready to serve, dish out on top of the toast, and sprinkle a bit of chopped parsley on top.

Try drinking chilled amontillado sherry with this. I know you're not an Oxford don but try it.

MUSHROOMS AND APPLES

Mushrooms and apples sound like a strange combination. I happened upon it because I was cooking some wild duck and the only vegetables I had were golf-ball sized button mushrooms. I also had some Cox's Orange Pippins which I was going to gently sauté by themselves with honey and ginger, something that goes well with game, pork or ham.

I decided to combine them and do them a different way. The end result blew my bananas off. I don't know why it worked so well but somehow we are back to our old friend umami. It made a wonderful combination with the duck and would have been good with any game or red meat.

It also makes a great starter served on a piece of sourdough toast.

Ingredients for four

+ 20 golf-ball sized button mushrooms, sliced not too thinly, say four slices per mushroom

+ 3 medium sized Cox's Orange Pippin apples (or similar firm, sweet-sharp, apples, not the awful French Golden Delicious), cut round the core into eight or so chunks with the skin still on.

+ Glug of rapeseed oil

+ 1 clove garlic finely chopped

+ 1 level tbsp sweet smoked paprika

+ 100ml dry white vermouth/fino sherry/white wine

+ Salt and pepper

What you do

Put the mushrooms and apples in a large frying pan or wok with the rapeseed oil over medium high heat. Sauté for five minutes until starting to soften. Add the paprika and sauté for another minute or so while mixing everything up. Add the vermouth and turn the heat up high to evaporate the vermouth. When the liquid is syrupy, after three or four minutes, reduce heat, season, and serve.

NORFOLK COUNTRY PÂTÉ

Everyone loves a pâté. French country-people eat pâté twice a week and few English country weekends go by without a pâté making an appearance. Remember an English sausage roll is a French pâté en croute. Pâtés, together with their first cousin the sausage have been around as long as cooking. There are a whole hierarchy of posh pâtés with foie gras sitting on top and other exotica lurking beneath, but, as is the case so often with cooking, and particularly with French cooking, it is the peasant housewife who has the best recipes. Pâté de foie gras is all very well, though perhaps not for the goose or duck that has donated its liver, but you would not want to eat it often or you would end up with a liver as swollen as the poor goose. It is almost pure fat.

You can, however, cheerfully tuck away pâté de campagne, country pâté, three or four times a week if you live in the Auvergne, or for that matter, in Norfolk. For some reason when you go to your neighbourhood deli in England, the pâté de campagne you find on sale will be Belgian. The Belgians are fine cooks and make a fine pâté but at heart this is a dish of the French countryside.

You can make a pâté out of almost any kind of meat and many kinds of fish, or even one of those toe-curling "vegetable terrines" or "mosaics" that were so popular in the 1990s. However, they are not pâté de campagne. A country pâté has pork in it. It has pig's liver in it. It has fat. It has alcohol. It has spices. That's about it.

It is easy to make, particularly if you follow my advice and get the butcher to do the yukky bit. Once he has ground the meat for you, you need to spend ten minutes or so mixing everything up, then you pop it in the oven, and, bing-bong-bang, ninety minutes later you take out a delicious pâté de campagne.

This is my recipe. It has elements stolen from Tamasin Day-Lewis and from the ever-wonderful Felicity Cloake, but I've given them both the Frank Sinatra treatment and done it My Way. It's good. You'll find the quantities below will feed fifteen or more people as a starter so I suggest you slice off as much as you need and freeze the rest. It freezes well.

"Pâtés, together with their first cousin the sausage have been around as long as cooking."

Ingredients for a small army (say, fifteen people)

Things to be minced together:

+ 500g belly pork, no rind

+ 350g unsmoked streaky bacon

+ 500g pig's liver

+ 200g pork back fat

+ ½ a pig's kidney

Note: mincing the five items above is not for the faint-hearted. The pig's liver in particular will bring out a touch of the squeams in anyone other than an axe-murderer or a butcher. Do not mince these things at home. You won't make a good job of it and it'll take for ever. And don't dream of putting it in your food processor. That will produce squodge, not mince. Ask your nice Mr Butcher to do it in his back room where he has an industrial strength mincer. It will take him three minutes. It might take you thirty.

Other Ingredients

+ Big knob of butter

+ 1 medium onion or two big shallots, finely chopped

+ 4 garlic cloves, crushed and chopped

+ 2 tsp chopped thyme, or 1 tsp dried

+ 2 tsp chopped rosemary, or 1 tsp dried

+ 2 tbsp green peppercorns

+ 1 tsp ground ginger

+ 1 tsp ground nutmeg

+ 1 tbsp juniper berries, squashed

+ 50g pistachios, roughly chopped

+ 100ml Calvados or Bourbon

+ 75ml dry white vermouth or dry sherry

+ 1 egg, beaten

+ Salt and black pepper

What you do

Gently fry the onions / shallots and garlic in the butter over low to medium heat till they are very soft, say ten to fifteen minutes. While that is happening get a giant bowl and add the other ingredients starting with the minced meat. Mix everything thoroughly, either with your hands or with a couple of big forks. By this time, the onions / shallots should be ready. Add them, give everything a giant grind of black pepper and a teaspoon of salt, depending on how salty your bacon is, and mix well again. Fry a small blob of mixture to test by tasting and adjust the seasoning.

You will now have about 2 litres of mixture. I spread this among two or three baking tins, maybe one 1 litre and two 500ml. You could use two 1 litre ones if you prefer. Of course, if you have them, you can use proper ceramic terrines. Most people line the baking tins with streaky bacon and cover the mixture with more bacon on top so that it is entirely wrapped. I don't. Yes, this does make it slightly easier to get out of the tins, but cold flabby, fatty, bacon is not a good taste to wrap your delicious terrine in. There is plenty of fat in the mixture which will melt during cooking and act as a lubricant. You don't need the bacon.

Heat your oven to 150c. Get a roasting tin, put the filled baking tins in it, having covered them with a tight foil lid, pour boiling water two-thirds of the way up the roasting tin and slide it into the middle of the oven. After an hour remove the foil lid and cook for another 20 minutes. Take out a *terrine* and test by sliding a metal skewer into the middle, taking it out after ten seconds, waiting a couple of moments, and then testing with your tongue. It should be warm to hot. If it's not, cook till it is.

Put a strip of foil down the terrine and balance weights or something heavy like tins of food on top to weight the terrine down. This will make it compact and sliceable, rather than loose and crumbly. Leave the terrine in a cool place till it's a suitable temperature to go in the refrigerator, still with the weights on top. Leave in the fridge for 24 hours, then take it out, slide a knife round the edge of the terrine, turn it upside down on to a handsome plate and shake. The terrine should come out on your plate, ready to serve when it has lost its fridge chill. Crusty sourdough, toast fingers, and cornichons are good accompaniments.

CHANTERELLE RISOTTO

If you're not a chanterelle-forager, you can find fresh ones quite easily in London. They are my second favourite mushroom, after morels, but morels cost more than caviar. If you're too lazy to make a risotto, chanterelles are delicious simply sautéed over medium heat in butter for a few minutes. I add a splosh of fino sherry, a wee squeeze of lemon juice, and some chopped parsley before serving on a bit of sourdough toast. Makes a good starter. However, chanterelle risotto is even better. If you can't get fresh chanterelles, this risotto is delicious with dried. If using dried, I use a mixture of dried chanterelles and dried morels. If you can afford them. Soak those in warm water before you cook them. Then take them out, squeeze them dry, and chop them up but keep the water the mushrooms have soaked in. Use it for the risotto instead of the chicken stock or use half chicken, half mushroom stock.

A word about risottos. Most recipes tell you to use olive oil and butter. Risottos come from northern Italy, particularly Venice. Venice is at heart a butter town not an olive oil one. We're not in Rome or Naples. By all means use half olive oil if you want. I just use butter. Tastes richer.

Booze. For this recipe I suggest rich, dark Madeira. You can add a number of alcohols when making a good risotto. For light risottos dry white vermouth is best; fino sherry is good; white wine works. Here I use Madeira to give this risotto an autumn evening, candle-light, feel but I would use vermouth in the spring. Some people find the Madeira makes the risotto too sweet and unctuous. If you're not keen on unctuosity stick to vermouth or sherry. And if you're using dried mushrooms then don't use Madeira, it would be too much with the darkness of the mushroom stock.

People have told me that this is the perfect dish for a seduction supper. I'm hoping you will tell me if that is true.

> "People have told me that this is the perfect dish for a seduction supper. I'm hoping you will tell me if that is true."

Ingredients for risotto for two

+ Full punnet of fresh chanterelles

+ 500ml chicken stock

+ 150g of risotto rice (make it 200g if you're feeling greedy)

+ 1 onion, finely chopped

+ Stick of celery, diced small

+ 2 cloves garlic, finely chopped

+ Handful of lardons from pancetta (Italians might leave out the lardons but I like them)

+ 100ml rich Madeira or sweet sherry

+ Parsley, lemon juice, parmesan, butter

+ Salt and pepper

What you do

First, cook your chanterelles. Toss them around in a sauté pan over medium heat with a blob of butter and a squeeze of lemon juice for five minutes, then keep them warm while you make the risotto.

Take a sauté pan about a foot across. Add a big blob of butter, sauté the onions, lardons, garlic and celery over medium heat till onions are soft and sweet, but not browned. Add the rice spread out on top. Pour in the Madeira, whack the heat right up, and bubble hard for two or three minutes while stirring. The smell of evaporating Madeira is heady.

Turn heat down to medium-low. The longer you take to cook your risotto the creamier it will be. Add a ladle or so of stock, which you have been keeping warm in a separate saucepan. It must be warm; if it's cold it will stop the rice cooking.

Stir gently. This is one of those things like scrambled eggs which need constant stirring. You'll find the stirring is quite Zen. When the first ladle has been absorbed, add another ladle and so on. After ten minutes of stirring, add your chanterelles which you have been keeping warm. Somewhere between fifteen and twenty minutes after you began stirring, you will find, on tasting a few grains of rice, that they are soft and creamy with a tiny bite of firmness in the middle. Perfect. Season with salt and pepper. If you run out of stock before the rice is ready, use hot water.

Turn off the heat and put a tight-fitting lid on the pan, or foil if you don't have a lid, and leave it to sit quietly while you finish your vodka martini with a few pistachios. After three minutes sitting undisturbed, remove the lid, throw in some chopped parsley, flat or curly, on top and serve on warm plates with a good grate of parmesan.

There is something about this kind of risotto. People say that oysters are an aphrodisiac. Maybe, but for a seduction supper, chanterelle or truffle risotto is numero uno. For best results, drink fridge-cold Madeira instead of wine with the risotto. I like Blandy's Duke of Clarence, named after the poor bastard who was drowned in 1478 in a butt of Malmsey (i.e. Madeira) on the orders of Edward IV who had been put up to it by his dodgy brother, later Richard III. If you don't get lucky after a supper of chanterelle risotto accompanied by rich, dark, Madeira, then you'd better stick to Tinder.

THREE HELPINGS SALAD

My favourite starter at a dinner for eight or more people is charcuterie. Cover a couple of big wooden boards with mounds of sliced iberico ham, mortadella, thinly-sliced salami, radishes, maybe a slab of **Norfolk Country Pate (see p. 28)**, and a bowl of cornichons. Serve that with country bread and butter. Not only does this taste good but people use their hands to eat, always a good way of making people unwind.

In these health-conscious days there are people who don't want to kick off their dinner with mounds of cured and salted piggy. The loss is theirs but some of them are my friends and they come to dinner.

Now I give them my **Three Helpings Salad**. Actually I give it to everyone. It is simple to make and unbelievably good. It acquired its name because even the men go back for second helpings and many for thirds. Not a leaf will be left over.

First, a word about lettuce in a salad. Please, no iceberg lettuce. Iceberg may have its uses as a wrapping for crispy duck or propping up something soggy in a prawn cocktail but it has as much flavour as wrapping paper. If you're making a salad as a starter as opposed to a green salad to go with a steak, you want to stick to lettuces that stay crisp but have some taste. I use cos (aka romaine) with some little gem. Then I pop off to Waitrose and buy a bag or two of their Crispy Mixed Salad or assorted Baby Leaves.

Ingredients for four

+ 2 cos lettuces

+ 4 little gem lettuces

+ 2 bags of crisp mixed salad including baby leaves

+ 2 endives, preferably the pink-edged ones

+ 2 fennel bulbs

+ 2 medium sized zucchini

+ 150g Roquefort

+ 2 pears, ripe but still crisp

+ Bunch of radishes, preferably the long thin ones.

+ 150ml *Mustard Vinaigrette (p.171)*

+ 100g chopped walnuts

What you do

Get a big serving platter. Cut the ends off the endives, separate the leaves, and scatter them over the plate. Tear up, don't cut, the cos and little gem lettuces into bite-size pieces and scatter. Pour the contents of the mixed leaf salads on to the plate.

Peel the pears and slice them vertically. Add to the plate. Using a peeler, slice the zucchini lengthwise into paper-thin slices. Add them to the salad. Slice the fennel bulbs across the bulb into very thin slices, removing the hard core, and chop, before spreading over the salad. Unwrap the Roquefort and, using your hands, crumble it all over the salad. Slice the radishes into thin rounds and add.

Mix everything up with your hands.

Put all the ingredients of the dressing, other than the walnuts, into a jam-jar or food container. Add salt and pepper. Shake vigorously and taste for oil-vinegar balance, adjusting if necessary. Add the walnuts to the dressing and give a shake.

Just before you serve, pour the vinaigrette over the salad, and give it a toss. Your guests will go on helping themselves till there is none left.

BURNT
GARLICKY
MUSHROOMS

Is there anyone who doesn't like a mushroom? There are of course an infinite variety of mushrooms and I have recipes elsewhere involving wonderful things like chanterelles and morels. However, the basic button mushroom is astonishingly versatile. It doesn't have a pronounced taste as such, although there is always a hint of umami about it, but it is brilliant at absorbing the flavours from the pan it is cooked in.

This recipe is one of my favourite starters. Everyone loves it but you should be warned that it is garlicky. Not a recipe to have the night before an exciting first date. The garlic and the mushrooms are cooked separately because you don't want to make the garlic bitter by burning it whereas you do want to give the mushrooms a brief scorching.

Ingredients for four

+ 500g button mushrooms, sliced thinly

+ 4 fat garlic cloves, chopped

+ 4 rashers streaky bacon cut into thin strips

+ 150ml sweet sherry or Madeira

+ Vegetable oil

+ Salt and pepper

+ 4 rounds of toast

What you do

Put a generous dash of oil in a big sauté pan over medium-low heat. Add the garlic and bacon. Leave them to cook gently for ten minutes or so, giving them an occasional stir. The garlic should go golden but not dark while the bacon renders much of its fat.

Take the garlic and bacon out and reserve, leaving the oil in the pan. There should be a couple of tablespoons. Turn the heat up to very high. Throw in the mushrooms and stir while allowing them to pick up the heat and start to go deep brown. You want them to be slightly burnt but not blackened. This will take about two minutes and the mushrooms will halve in size as they give up their moisture. Add the sherry or Madeira, keeping the heat high so that the liquid bubbles away and reduces. When the liquid is about to turn syrupy, lower the heat to medium-low and add back the garlic and bacon. Give a good grind of salt and pepper. Stir well.

Spoon the mushrooms out on to rounds of toast, trying to give everyone some of the syrupy juice, and serve on hot plates.

MENORCAN MUSHROOMS

You will of course find these mushrooms all over Spain; I call them Menorcan mushrooms because I ate so many of them one night in Mahon that I smelled like a garlic factory for the next week. And, by the way, if you're curious where the word 'mayonnaise' came from, look no further than Port Mahon, the capital of Menorca and the place where Nelson kept Lady Hamilton in a house by the harbour where she could look out to sea and wait for him to come home.

When the French conquered Menorca in the 18th century, as so many other people did before and after them, they found an island where cream was in short supply but they also found that the locals had perfected the creamiest of sauces using olive oil and egg yolks; no cream, much like carbonara sauce. There were few things to match a Menorcan prawn dipped in the local oil and egg sauce. The French loved it and adopted it as a key part of French cuisine. They called it after the place they had discovered it, Sauce Mahonaise, although they Frenchified the spelling.

Getting back to the mushrooms. In Spain they are served as tapas. In England I serve them on sourdough toast as the simplest and best of starters. You won't believe how good these taste. These are similar to my *Burnt Garlicky Mushrooms (see p. 34)* but, while those are almost brutal, these are more sophisticated. To a degree...

Ingredients for four

+ 20 button mushrooms, stalks removed
+ Olive oil
+ 3 garlic cloves, finely chopped
+ Teaspoon of sweet paprika
+ 4 spring onions, finely chopped, green bits only
+ 100ml dry sherry
+ 4 slices sourdough toast

What you do

Slice the mushrooms thinly. Add a glug of olive oil to a frying pan on a medium to hot heat. Throw in the mushrooms and poke them around with a wooden spatula. As they start to colour add the garlic. You want the garlic to keep a touch of rawness to give the mushrooms an old-fashioned Spanish bite. Add the spring onion green bits. In Spain they're more likely to add parsley but onions add more flavour.

Add the sherry and turn the heat up to a hot sizzle to evaporate the liquid which shouldn't take more than a minute or two. As it's starting to evaporate, add the paprika. Stir everything around furiously and lower the heat right down as the sherry evaporates leaving a syrupy residue.

Spoon over sourdough toast on four warmed plates. Cut the toast into smaller pieces and eat in your fingers.

CRAB WITH CIDER

This is another recipe, along with **Claudia's Lobster Hotpot (see p. 66)**, inspired by Claudia Roden's *The Food of Spain*. Thank you, Claudia.

Claudia's version comes from Asturias and is made with their famous spider crab, the *txangurro*. My version doesn't use *txangurro* but the British brown crab. You could serve this dish in a ramekin but don't. If you are using fresh crab, you will have a crab shell. Serve it in that. And if you are not using fresh crab in the shell, then please don't make this dish.

Asturias, the northern part of Spain between Galicia and the Basque country, is rainy, green, apple-growing, country. Asturias, like those other Celtic lands, Cornwall and Brittany, makes excellent cider. Asturian cider is hard and dry. If you are using West Country cider make sure you get one that is dry.

Ingredients for four

+ 1 medium onion, chopped
+ 2 tbsp olive oil
+ 1 medium tomato, finely chopped
+ 1 tsp chilli flakes
+ 500g cooked white and dark crab meat, well mixed
+ 175ml dry cider
+ 2 tbsp chopped flat-leaf parsley
+ 2 tbsp fine breadcrumbs (I use Panko)
+ 15g butter, cut into small pieces
+ Salt and pepper

What you do

In a large frying pan, sauté the onion in the oil over a low to medium heat, stirring occasionally, until soft. Add the tomato and the chilli flakes, season with salt and black pepper and cook over medium heat for about eight minutes without browning the onion.

Add the crab meat, cider, and parsley to the pan. Mix gently and cook for one minute more. Spoon the crab mixture into the crab shells. Sprinkle the tops with the breadcrumbs and dot with butter, then put the shells under the grill until lightly brown.

Eat this with a slice of country bread and drink what remains of the cider to accompany it.

DUCK CONFIT SALAD

Confit duck legs are one of the best larder foods. You can confit the legs yourself at home but the bought ones in a jar or vacuum-sealed are so good that your home-made ones may not match them. As long as they are well-sealed, they will last for a long time. How easy it is to whip them out, spend a minimum of time preparing them, and turn them into something both elegant and inviting. This salad makes a good light lunch dish or a starter at dinner.

Ingredients for four

+ 2 confit duck legs
+ 200g chopped pancetta or lardons
+ 300g salad leaves, such as frisée, radicchio, lamb's lettuce
+ 1 crisp apple, Cox's Orange Pippins are best
+ 100ml *mustard vinaigrette (see p.171)*
+ 100g chopped walnuts
+ Salt and pepper

What you do

Fry the duck legs over medium heat for 15 minutes till the skin is crisp. Add the lardons to cook with them in the duck fat for the last five minutes.

Arrange the salad leaves on a plate in a mound. Shred the duck leg with a fork or your fingers. Mix the duck shreds and lardons with the salad. Chop up the apple into small pieces and add to the salad.

Mix the walnut pieces with the vinaigrette and pour it over the salad. Add salt and pepper. Mix well and serve.

THE RECTOR'S COCKLES

Two villages west of my village of Blakeney on the Norfolk coast is the village of Stiffkey*. Incoming Londoners pronounce it Stewkey because that's how they think the locals say it. All the locals I know pronounce it Stiffkey but they may have reverted to that pronunciation to make the incoming Londoners look stupid.

What is not under debate is that Stiffkey produces the finest cockles in the land and that, owing to some local quirk of geology, something about chalk in the marshes, they are a delightful blue colour. However you pronounce the village, the cockles are always called Stewkey Blues.

For this recipe you need to go out at low tide beyond the Stiffkey Marshes and dig around for cockles with your toes and a small spade. Failing that you can go to your fishmonger and buy some fresh cockles from him, or clams, the *palourde* type, or even mussels. This recipe works well with all three. It makes a great starter.

*Stiffkey is famous for two things, the Stewkey Blue cockles and for Harold Davidson, the Rector of Stiffkey. In the 1930s he used to take time off from ministering to the good people of Stiffkey to catch the train to London and minister to teenage prostitutes whom he would befriend in the West End. Some he asked home with him. At times there were up to twenty hookers spending the night in the Rectory under the Rev Davidson's ministrations. The locals complained to the Bishop of Norwich and after a highly public trial, the Rector was defrocked for immorality. He became a circus performer. His party piece was to enter a cage, dressed in the rectorial garb to which he was no longer entitled, with two lions in it, give them a ringing sermon and command them, when he put his head in their mouths, to do him no harm. The lions were tame and placid beasts until one, tiring of the sermon, bit the Rector of Stiffkey's head off till it was left hanging by the windpipe. He was rushed to hospital where he died, not because of his semi-detached head, but apparently because of an overdose of insulin. Huh? Look the story up on Wikipedia under Rector of Stiffkey. There is much more to it than I have room for here.

Ingredients for four

+ Four handfuls of Stewkey Blues (or fresh, live, clams or mussels)
+ Eight fresh unpeeled, uncooked, big prawns, three or four inches long
+ Four garlic cloves, finely chopped
+ 100ml breadcrumbs
+ Cup of dry white vermouth, fino sherry, or white wine
+ Shot of Pernod
+ Chilli flakes
+ 4 spring onions, finely chopped
+ Cup of coriander leaves, well chopped
+ Oil, butter, lemon

What you do

Add a good glug of olive oil and a slug of butter to a big frying pan on medium heat. Toss in the garlic, add a flat teaspoon of chilli flakes, and cook for five minutes, stirring from time to time. Pour in the breadcrumbs and turn up the heat to medium-high. You want to make the breadcrumbs golden not black. This should take five minutes but keep moving the crumbs around the pan.

Add the Stewkey Blues and the prawns, add the vermouth, Pernod, and an equivalent amount of water, and turn the heat up so everything comes to a bubble. Give the cockles and prawns a good mixing up. Put a lid on the pan for three minutes. Take the lid off and throw in the spring onions and coriander. Keep it bubbling away for another couple of minutes and then dish out into bowls. Eat with your fingers and a spoon for the liquid.

EEL AND ENDIVE SALAD

I love smoked eel. People who blench at the thought of eating eel imagine it to be slimy and fishy. It is neither, but firm of flesh and not a hint of fishiness about it. As with so many fish, eels in Europe have been brought to the edge of extinction, so make sure you buy your eels from someone who is responsible about harvesting them.

I like to buy whole smoked eels and chop them up myself. Skinning an eel and removing the fillets from the spine is not difficult and gratifyingly satisfying. Or you can buy smoked eel fillets from a good supplier.

Of course, the person who has done most to introduce sceptical Londoners to the wonder of smoked eel is the great Jeremy Lee, chef and co-owner of Quo Vadis in Dean Street, the home of his Smoked Eel Sandwich, possibly the best starter in London…

Ingredients for six

+ 6 endives, regular or pink
+ 2 cups smoked eel, filleted and chopped into little finger-sized lengths
+ 2 handfuls of frisée
+ 100ml *mustard vinaigrette (see p.171)*
+ 100g chopped walnuts

What you do

Separate the endives into individual leaves (you'll need to cut the base off so they come free). Add the smoked eel fillets and frisée. Mix by hand and divide equally between the plates.

Put the dressing ingredients in a jam-jar or small food container. Give it a grind of salt and pepper. Add the walnuts. Shake vigorously.

Pour dressing over salad just before serving.

SLOTTED PIMPS

Many things define English food, some such as kippers and mushy peas are confusing to a foreigner, some, (hello boiled landlady cabbage), outright disgusting, and some sublime but little known outside England. We can debate what belongs on the sublime list; spotted dick and custard? Toad in the hole? Pork pies? Treacle tart? Eccles cakes? Cottage pie? Steak and kidney pudding?

There is however one dish that everyone agrees is sublimity itself, the quintessence of Englishness, the High Priest of high tea, yes, potted shrimps, or slotted pimps as they are more generally known.

They need to be warm and buttery and preferably reside on a warm crumpet just buttery enough to leak butter down your shirt-front.

People usually buy little cardboard tubs of slotted pimps in a shop but making them yourself is so simple and so much better that it is a pity not to do so. There is one drawback. A decent-sized pot of pimps might well have a hundred or more tiny pimplets in it. Someone has to peel those tiny animals. Long and boring work. The best solution is to do what I do. Find a good local fishmonger. They do exist and they will be able to procure little peeled brown shrimps for you. Once you have done that the rest is simple. By the way, do not think for an instant about using those tiny white Icelandic frozen shrimps, the kind of thing you get in a hotel shrimp cocktail; they would not work. Nor would bigger shrimps. It's little peeled brown shrimps about the size of your thumbnail or nothing.

Although unpotted shrimps go off very quickly, the butter acts as a preservative so that the potted ones will keep happily for a week in the fridge. You can freeze these shrimps but be sure to take them out a long time in advance so they can thaw out properly. Don't refreeze them. They would be mushy.

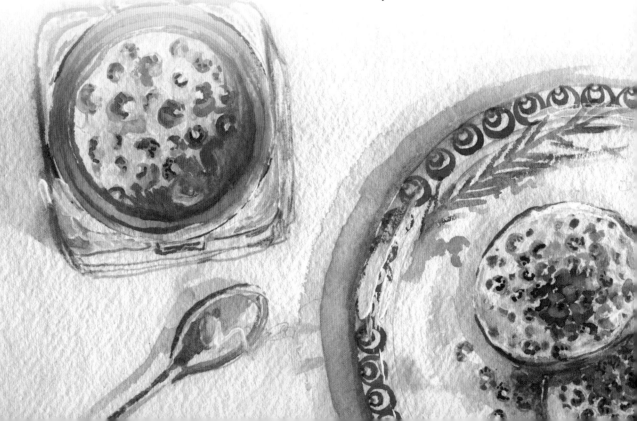

"There is however one dish that everyone agrees is sublimity itself, the quintessence of Englishness, the High Priest of high tea, yes, potted shrimps, or slotted pimps as they are more generally known."

Ingredients for a 500ml mason jar (enough to do about a dozen pimp-heaped crumpets)

+ 500g peeled and cooked brown shrimps

+ 500g salted butter (most recipe books tell you to use clarified butter, or unsalted butter, or to strain the butter through muslin; I use a good basic salted butter like Anchor, or Kerrygold and it works just fine)

+ 2 tsp nutmeg

+ 2 tsp ground ginger

+ (I use nutmeg and ginger but feel free to experiment and add the spices you like; both cinnamon and mace are good)

+ Squeeze of lemon

+ Big dash of tabasco

What you do

Heat the butter up over a low-to-medium heat but don't burn it. When it's liquid, add the other ingredients except for the shrimp and give it a good stir. Take off the heat.

Fill the jar a third full of shrimps. They should be room temperature. Pour in butter to cover and squelch around with a spoon to make sure the crannies are filled with butter. Repeat twice till the jar is full. You should have enough butter to completely cover the shrimps. If not, melt and season a bit

more and pour it on. Decorate with a sprig of rosemary, thyme or whatever you fancy on top of the butter. Close the lid and put in fridge as soon as it has cooled a bit.

To serve

You can eat them three ways.

The crumpet way. Toast crumpets and put one on each plate. Warm the shrimps in a frying pan or low oven just enough so the butter starts to melt but is not completely liquid. Spoon the shrimps on to the crumpets. You'll probably need a knife and fork to eat them unless you want a river of butter down your cashmere sweater.

The toast soldiers way. Make toast soldiers. I like good white sandwich bread but use wholemeal if you want. Put the mason jar in the middle of the table. It should be at room, not fridge, temperature. People spoon the pimps on to their plates, balance as many as they can on a toast finger, and eat.

The Robert Maxwell way. Robert Maxwell, the press baron who fell into disgrace and then off the back of a yacht, used to sit by himself in his office in the Mirror building in Fleet Street eating giant tins of caviar with a tea spoon. He'd shovel it in straight off the spoon, no blini, no sour cream, nothing additional. I have been known to do this with slotted pimps. I have been known to do this with slotted pimps, warmed enough so the butter is melty and shovelled them in with a teaspoon.

Something Eggy

Many years ago I was lucky enough to be invited by an American business friend on an amazing trip to India. We spent a week in Rajasthan hobnobbing with maharajas and going to all-night feasts in floodlit palaces. We ended up back in Delhi at a posh hotel, exhausted by a week of long journeys and late nights.

My wife, Guislaine, and I found ourselves sharing the lift down at 6:30 pm with the author John Julius Norwich and his wife who were also on the trip. "What are we doing tonight?" said John Julius. "Apparently," said Guislaine, "they are putting us in buses and taking us off to a special son et lumiere performance at the Red Fort.

"What wouldn't I give," said John Julius with a giant sigh, "to stay in our room and have something eggy in front of the television."

BEST BREAKFAST OMELETTE

Diets… dontcha love them? Most of us have tried most of them. You would think that science could tell us how to lose weight. It's alarming to find how uncertain science is on so many things. Losing weight is one of them. Everyone swears by their own particular way which contradicts everyone else's way. Through most of my lifetime doctors have told you to cut calories as the only way of losing weight and then up popped Mr Atkins, resuscitating the old Victorian Banting diet, and saying that counting calories was irrelevant. Cutting out carbs was what you should do. Go ahead, eat as much fat as you like. Butter, olive oil, full cream are terrific to taste and good for you. But keep off the bread and pasta. Meanwhile, the government's Health Adviser is telling you that butter and cream will give you a heart attack and make you obese. I wouldn't believe anything a government health adviser told me on principle and recently even they have been modifying their position. Remember how health-giving orange juice is now toxic according to the health nazis?

A year ago, a wonderful woman called Sabine, who looks and behaves like Superwoman, set up a WhatsApp group for three men she knew whom she'd seen at a big party. She said, "Guys, you are all good looking men. But you've let yourselves go. If you want to get back in shape I'll tell you how to do it. I let myself go but then decided to do something about it. I've lost 12 kilos And I feel terrific."

I was one of those men. We signed up with Mistress Sabine. She was clear. Cut out the carbs and the weight would fall away. Even better you would not feel hungry. Reader, it works. If you are interested Google keto or low-carb diets and they will tell you what to do.

There is a problem though with low-carb. Breakfast. Yes, you can eat as many eggs as you like. You can pile on the bacon. But you can't have a piece of toast. Eating an egg with no toast is no fun. Unless you make it into an omelette. Try this for breakfast. Or for a light lunch or supper. It's ridiculously good and ridiculously healthy. It's more of a frittata than an omelette.

Ingredients for two

+ 4 rashers of streaky bacon, chopped
+ 4 spring onions, chopped
+ 5 eggs
+ 100ml double cream
+ Big handful of fresh spinach
+ 100g parmesan chopped small
+ Knob of butter
+ Salt and pepper

What you do

Take a medium-sized pan and fry the bacon and spring onions over medium heat for three minutes. Throw in the spinach and cook very briefly until the spinach just starts to wilt but no more. Remove bacon, onions and spinach to a plate. Pour off the bacon fat.

Beat the eggs with a fork. Remove the pan from the heat. Add a good knob of butter and pour in the eggs. Spread the bacon, onions and spinach on top. Cook until the edges start to firm, about five minutes depending on the heat. Sprinkle the parmesan over it. Dribble the cream out over the top. Add salt and pepper and put under a hot grill until the cheese has melted and the top is starting to puff and brown. That should take around five minutes. I have been known to add sliced sausage or chorizo to the top of this.

> "Eating an egg with no toast is no fun. Unless you make it into an omelette."

PIP-PIP PIPERADE

There is a reason why there are more three-star restaurants around San Sebastian than any other provincial town in Europe. The Basques. The Basques may be argumentative and dodgy people. These are the guys at whose hands Charlemagne suffered his only defeat. He had been pootling around Spain subduing the odd Moor and decided eventually to return to France where some northerners were revolting. Legend and *le Chanson de Roland* have it that Charlemagne's army was attacked by 400,000 crazed Moors. The truth was that the Moors were snoozing on the Costa Brava when his army crossed the high Pyrenees over the Roncesvalles pass, but a relatively small army of stroppy Basques, annoyed because Charlemagne had knocked down Pamplona's walls, set upon his rear-guard, commanded by the immortal Roland, and slaughtered them to the last man, including the no-longer-so-immortal Roland. Stroppy the Basques may be but when it comes to cooking they have perfect pitch. You won't spend a better evening than having a tapas-crawl round San Sebastian or Logrono.

Piperade is not really restaurant food. It doesn't look pretty, a yellowy-brown glop with bits in it, but it does taste good. Pure comfort food. It's what the Basques eat when they are staying home watching pelota on the telly and so should you. Healthy, easy to make, and like so many peasant dishes, the ingredients are flexible and depend on what you have in your larder.

I add potatoes to my piperade, something a Basque would never do but I can't think why not. They are a good textural counterpart to the other vegetables.

Ingredients for four

+ 3 decent-sized onions, sliced into strips but not diced

+ 400g tomatoes (If your veg-supplier only has Dutch or English unripe tomatoes, use canned ones, at least they were canned when ripe, but pour away half the liquid)

+ 3 bell peppers, preferably different colours including green, cut into inch-long strips

+ 300g lardons

+ 300g waxy potatoes cut into small cubes

+ 4 spring onions chopped into half-inch pieces

+ 2 cloves garlic, chopped

+ Chopped fresh herbs, whatever you like – thyme, rosemary or basil are good.

+ 6 eggs, lightly beaten.

+ Olive oil and, to taste, pepper, salt and a pinch of chilli flakes.

What you do

Put a big frying pan or wok on medium heat and add a glug of olive oil. Sauté the onions until they are starting to soften but not brown, then add the peppers, garlic, tomatoes, potatoes, and lardons. Add herbs and season with salt, pepper, and chilli flakes. Cook over medium heat stirring with a wooden spatula from time to time. Putting a lid on for half the time speeds up the cooking process. After fifteen to twenty minutes take out some bits and taste. The onion and tomato should be soft but the peppers and potatoes should still have some firmness. When ready, add the spring onions followed by the eggs. Now stir quickly as with scrambled eggs. The eggs will cook in a matter of seconds. You want to keep them softish. Give the mixture a good grind of salt and pepper.

Remove from heat to stop further cooking and spoon out on to warm plates. Eat with good crusty bread, fresh or toasted.

The Basques usually serve with thin Bayonne ham slices or maybe some sliced salami. Both are fine but I prefer just the lardons cooked with the piperade.

If ever a dish cried out for Rioja it is this.

ONION OMELETTE

Many years ago I was ski-ing with friends in Val d'Isere. To get away from the crowds we were ski-ing from Le Fornet, a tiny village a short way up the valley with its own lift connecting up with the main lift network. We stopped for lunch at the mid-station restaurant which one of my friends knew well. It was a sit-down, waitress-service place with blue checked tablecloths. "Try the onion omelette, you'll love it," my friend said. I had never had an onion omelette before so I did. It was one of the best simple things I had ever eaten. A wonderful combination of sweet onion and runny omelette as only the French do them. If you want a simple, light, supper, there's nothing better than this with a green salad and a cool glass of Beaujolais.

Recently I discovered that I was not the only person with a liking for an omelette aux oignons. In Waverley Root's magisterial *The Food of France* he tells how Louis XIII, the 17th century French king who preferred to hunt at the royal chateau of Amboise while Richelieu got on with running France, also liked to cook. "His tastes were simple," says Root. "What he usually made for himself was an onion omelette, sometimes moistened with a little red wine." I haven't tried moistening my onion omelette with red wine but, if you do, let me know how it tastes.

Ingredients for one

+ 1 large or 2 small onions, sliced into shreds

+ 3 eggs

+ Butter

+ Salt and pepper

What you do

Heat an omelette pan to medium-low, put in a good splodge of butter and the sliced onion. Cook gently with an occasional stir. Don't hurry and don't let the onions burn. It will take up to thirty minutes but any attempt to shorten the time will ruin the onions for this dish. When the onions are soft and caramelly, slide them on to a plate to stay warm.

Beat your eggs with a fork. Turn the heat up to medium-high, add another good splodge of butter. If the heat is right it should sizzle but not burn. Pour in the eggs, add the onions in a line along the middle of the eggs, and make your omelette the usual way by lifting the edges to let the liquid run underneath. When the omelette surface is still a little runny, or *baveuse* as the French say, flip one edge over the middle and then the other, slide the omelette on to a warm plate, season with salt and pepper, pour a glass of wine and eat while it's still hot.

FRITTATA: THE NO DOUGH PIZZA

Everyone loves pizza, possibly the world's most universal food. Sadly it is also one of the most fattening. There is no substitute for a pizza as the dough, whether it's soft and puffy or thin and crispy, is exquisite. However frittata is a close runner-up and a million times healthier.

There are an infinite amount of frittatas, as you can put just about anything on top. In my experience the best ones, like the best pizzas, don't have too much on top. All a frittata needs is a vegetable, some cured meat, and some cheese. There should never be so much topping that you can't see the egg underneath. Better too little than too much. Here is a favourite frittata below. Feel free to substitute as much as you like but try to keep the vegetable/meat/trio intact.

> "There are an infinite amount of frittatas, as you can put just about anything on top. In my experience the best ones, like the best pizzas, don't have too much on top."

Ingredients for three to four

+ 8 eggs
+ Butter
+ 2 large or 3 small shallots chopped
+ 2 cloves garlic
+ 4 spring onions chopped
+ 100g peas, frozen are fine
+ 4 rashers streaky bacon chopped to matchsticks
+ 200g parmesan chopped small
+ 3 tbsp double cream or crème fraiche
+ Salt and pepper

What you do

Beat the eggs well with a fork. Set aside. Turn on your overhead grill to high.

Put a 30cm frying pan on medium heat. Add the butter followed by the shallots and garlic. Cook till soft but not coloured, about seven minutes. Add the spring onions, peas, and bacon. Cook, stirring from time to time, for another five minutes.

Turn the heat up to medium-high and pour in the eggs making sure the toppings are well-distributed. Sprinkle the parmesan over the top. Give everything a good grind of salt and pepper. Cook until the edges are firming up but the middle is still runny. Spoon the cream over the top.

Take the pan off the hob and slide it under the grill about 10cm away. Watch carefully. In a few minutes the cheese will be melting and the surface will be puffing up. Wait till the frittata is on the edge of charring and remove just before it does,

Slice like pizza and serve on warm plates. A green salad goes well with this. And if there are only two of you so there's some left over, pop it in the fridge and eat it the next day.

WELSHMEN ON HORSEBACK

This got its name because I start with a Welsh rarebit and then load it with some of my favourite things. This is the ultimate umami-laden comfort food. It makes a perfect light supper, accompanied by the remains of the beer that went into the recipe. Maybe a green salad too.

Ingredients for two

+ 150g grated hard cheese, preferably English, cheddar is good

+ 2 tbsp stout, ale if you don't have stout, lager at a pinch

+ Good dash of Worcester sauce

+ 1 tsp Dijon mustard (or English if you prefer)

+ 8 fillets salted anchovies

+ 2 eggs

+ 2 slices good white bread

What you do

Mix the cheese, stout, Worcester sauce and mustard in a bowl. Meanwhile turn your grill to high and toast the slices of bread.

Spread the cheese mixture on top of the toast and put under the grill. Watch carefully as it won't take long. When you see the cheese starting to bubble up and go brown, remove from the grill. Spread four anchovy fillets on each Welshman in a lattice pattern. Put them in a warming drawer while you quickly fry two eggs.

Place an egg on top of each Welshman and serve immediately.

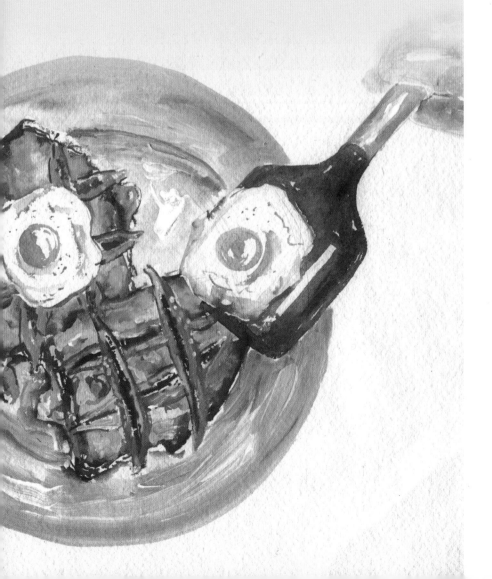

Soups

I have been accused of being overly soupist. There may be truth in this. Soups are a thing of infinite variety, hot and warming in December, chilly and cooling in July, full of substance and depth with vegetables and rich stock, or as delicate as the lightest consommé. Soups are wonderfully accommodating. You can take any of my recipes and add your own inspirations to make an even better soup. Far from objecting, I will applaud. I have also been accused, with equal truth, of being overly fish soupist. Guilty as charged. When I have people to dinner, as often as not, I give them a fish soup. Yes, there are a number of fish soup recipes here. Please try them all. I think you will love them as much as I do.

EL MILO'S
GAZPACHO

Most gazpachos and indeed most vegetable soups are ruined by the food processor. The food processor is the Donald Trump of the kitchen battery. Everyone now owns one and they use it to turn delicious traditional soups into baby food. I love Italian minestrones with chunks of vegetables crowding out the liquid. Put it in a Magimix and all you have is baby food.

With gazpacho it is the same. Order it in a restaurant and you are presented with a plate of orange puree. When Spanish peasant women first made gazpacho, the food processor had not been invented. Their only kitchen appliance was a razor-sharp Spanish knife. They used this to chop the ingredients into a fine dice. Then they used their fingers to tear the bread into small chunks, added the liquids, mixed it all up with their hands and left it to sit in a cool place overnight or longer. That is how you make gazpacho. The expression "mouth feel" sounds creepy but you will find that this gazpacho has a very different mouth feel to the purées.

"Most gazpachos and indeed most vegetable soups are ruined by the food processor. The food processor is the Donald Trump of the kitchen battery."

Ingredients for eight

+ 12 inches of cucumber

+ A big red onion or use shallots instead, finely chopped

+ 5 finely chopped spring onions

+ 2 garlic cloves, sliced fine

+ 4 slices of day-old good quality white bread with not quite all the crust removed

+ 6 tomatoes, they must be truly ripe, otherwise substitute for half of them a can of chopped tomatoes

+ 2 bell peppers, one of them red, chopped small

+ 100ml olive oil

+ 50ml of wine vinegar

+ 500ml tomato juice or good Bloody Mary mix

+ 100ml fino sherry

+ Big handful of chopped coriander

+ Juice of a lemon

+ A few dashes of Tabasco

+ 1 tsp sugar or more if your tomatoes are acid and unripe

+ Season with salt and pepper

What you do

Peel the cucumbers, onion, and garlic. Chop the vegetables into a very small dice, preferably a quarter the size of a sugar cube. Shred the bread into small pieces. Put them all together in a big bowl.

Separately mix the olive oil, vinegar, tomato juice, coriander, lemon juice, Tabasco, and sugar.

Pour this over the vegetables and mix it all up with your hands.

Put this to chill in the fridge at least overnight if you can. Next day give it a taste and adjust seasoning, sugar, vinegar, tabasco if necessary. Put in bowls, drizzle with more olive oil and serve with an ice-cold glass of albarino or, even better, fino sherry.

GASCON GARBURE

In 1989, Guislaine, my long-suffering then wife, and I walked across France. I had just chucked up my job after 22 years shouting down a phone as an investment banker, and the world before us was as open and unmarked as the Pacific Ocean. Before thinking of how to earn a living, we bought a couple of back-packs and walked across France from the Mediterranean, near Narbonne, to the Atlantic, just North of Biarritz. We were unfit and unprepared and it was 550 kilometres, an unthinkably long way to go for two spoilt Londoners who needed instructions as to how to wear a back-pack. It turned to be one of the hottest months on record; we stayed in *gites* with homicidal proprietors and *pensions* which shook when every truck went past; we were chased by dogs; and our feet were soon bandaged like mummies. Inexplicably we loved it. Humankind is strange. (I wrote a book about our walk, *The Man Who Broke Out of the Bank*, which in 1993 inexplicably got to no 5 on the British best-seller list. Second-hand copies can still be found on Amazon.)

Southwest France has an admirable and distinctive cuisine. It's only problem is that it is more suited to Norway than France. In the torrid Aquitaine evenings we longed for salads, oysters and shrimps, grilled fish, fresh vegetables, and green herbs. What did we get? Cassoulet; confit de canard; magret de canard; foie gras; pigeon in red wine; duck gizzard salad... all things that you'd love when an icy gale was blowing outside. And to crown it all everything is cooked in goose or duck fat. The wine too, Corbieres, Cahors,

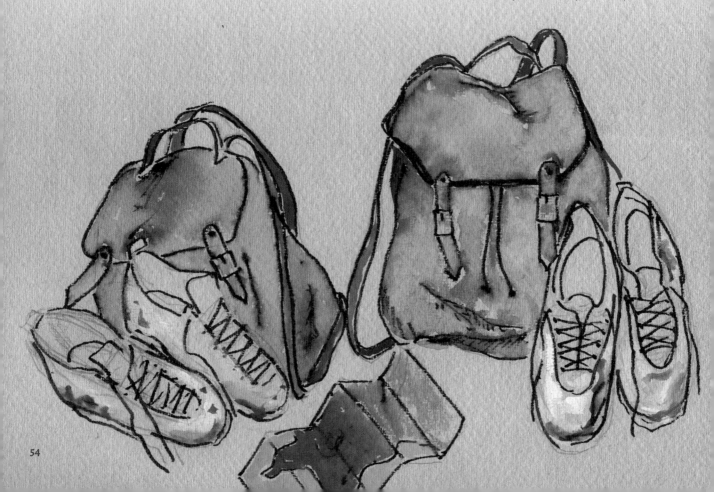

and Madiran, is powerful black stuff, delicious, but the kind of thing to add thigh muscle to a Gascon rugbyman, not to soothe a foot-weary Englishman's parched throat.

By the time we reached Samatan, roughly halfway across France, and home to one of the great foie gras markets, I was ready to join the Duck Liberation Front.

But there was one thing I grew to love that cropped up at almost every meal. It was seldom on the menu. It would just be automatically served, like bread, before your first course. You'd be sitting there waiting for the foie gras when the proprietor would shimmy up with two soup plates and a steaming tureen. He put the plates in front of you and ladled garbure into them. Garbure doesn't have an English name. "Cabbage soup with other vegetables and a bit of duck or pork or chicken" is the best translation. It's good. I have it for Sunday supper. A big plate of garbure and you need nothing else. You may wonder what the difference between garbure and potée is. Nothing. Same soup, different place.

As with cassoulet, there are as many recipes as there are kitchens in Gascony. Many have beans, confit de canard, leeks and whatever else is seasonally available. Feel free to add anything that seems right to you. The soup will love it.

Here's mine, a simple one but none the worse for that.

"Southwest France has an admirable and distinctive cuisine. It's only problem is that it is more suited to Norway than France."

Ingredients for four

+ 500g pancetta or streaky bacon cut into chunks
+ 1 onion and a couple of cloves of garlic, chopped
+ 3 carrots, chopped
+ 5 waxy new potatoes, chopped into cubes
+ 1l chicken stock
+ 1/2 head cabbage, chopped into postage stamp-sized pieces
+ 200g peas, frozen are fine
+ Half a wineglass of dry sherry

Optional but delicious extras:

+ A ham hock
+ A big chunk of parmesan rind, the great soup-enhancer beloved of every French and Italian housewife
+ Toulouse sausage, chopped into inch rounds, or even a couple of chopped frankfurters
+ Shredded left-over chicken or pheasant

What you do

Sweat the onion, garlic, carrots, and potatoes with some olive oil (duck fat if you have it) in a heavy-bottomed saucepan over a low-to-medium heat for ten minutes or so. Add the chicken stock. Simmer for twenty minutes.

Remove the pan and whiz the soup with a stick blender so it is about half whizzed but there are still plenty of individual pieces of vegetable. This gives the soup a good texture. Taste and add salt and pepper.

Add the pancetta, cabbage and peas along with the sherry. Simmer for another ten minutes and serve.

If you are a genuine Gascon you will wolf down two plates of garbure followed by a large bowl of cassoulet accompanied by a pint of inky Cahors wine, and maybe a few chunks of goat cheese. You will then go and play rugby for two hours.

HUNGARIAN COWBOY SOUP

Hungary is hot in summer and marrow-chilling in winter when the East wind howls in across the Great Hungarian Plain. The plain is a place of cattle; the cowboys who round them up, the famed Hungarian horsemen, are called *gulyas*. They need to keep warm in winter. Nothing does it better than a rib-sticking bowl of cowboy soup, or goulash as we pronounce *gulyas*.

Goulash was originally just chunks of beef stewed up with some water and a bit of potato and carrot, a Hungarian Irish stew substituting beef for mutton. Not very nice unless you were desperate. Then, some time in the 19th century, the Hungarians acquired a taste for a spice that they had known about for a couple of hundred years but had till then largely ignored. Paprika. Paprika went from being a little-used ingredient to a Hungarian obsession.

Peppers of course were unknown in Europe before the Americas were discovered. The Spanish were the first to import them and pretty soon *pimenton* in all its variety became a key part of Spanish cooking. Peppers spread along the Mediterranean seaways and were eagerly adopted in the Balkans, part then of the Ottoman Empire. The Turks loved them and began growing them in Croatia and introducing them to other parts of their empire. Although the Turks never really conquered the mountains of Hungary in the North, they held the whole of the plain and pretty soon its inhabitants were growing peppers. They called the peppers by their Serbo-Croatian name, *papar*, which soon became *paprika*, little pepper, in Hungarian.

To start with, paprika was hot, very hot, but, a hundred years ago, some clever Hungarian farmer found a sweet mutant breed of paprika and developed that. Today, if you go into the great Budapest market by the Chain Bridge, you will be confronted by marble slab on marble slab displaying foie gras (much of which is exported to France, put in cans, and rebranded as French), while hanging from every beam and festooning every pillar are ropes of brilliant red and yellow peppers, from the very hottest to the sweetest and mildest. Cowboy soup, meet paprika. What a marriage.

Of course, like so many country dishes, there is no "correct" version, any more than there is a correct version of cottage pie. You can put what you like in a goulash as long as it has meat and paprika. Traditionally, the meat is beef but Hungarians also make it with pork, lamb, or rabbit, and horse or donkey when times are hard. I make it with lamb because that has more flavour than beef and it's easier to keep tender but I don't use lamb stock as that would be a flavour step too far.

My biggest departure from most recipes you will find is that I don't use tomatoes. I love tomatoes. But since it's almost impossible to get a ripe tomato in a London shop, so I prefer, in cooking, to use canned tomatoes, canned when they are at their ripest. However, for my taste, people use tomatoes too much in stews. Tomatoes are wonderful but they do have an acid edge, even ripe ones. I don't want an acid edge in my stews and I don't want to have to add sugar or honey to counter the acidity. In a similar way, my ***Beantown Beans and Bangers (see p. 90)*** doesn't use tomatoes.

Juniper berries are my addition; I like their gaminess. As is the fino sherry which you won't find in a genuine goulash but which adds a fragrant zing to most soups.

Ingredients for four

+ 2 tbsp of lard or beef dripping (you can use olive or vegetable oil but it won't taste as mitteleuropean)

+ 1kg lamb leg steaks, say, 4 steaks, don't chop them up

+ 2 medium onions, chopped

+ 2 carrots, chopped

+ 1 stick celery, chopped

+ 3 cloves garlic, chopped

+ 1 tbsp sweet smoked paprika

+ 1 tbsp caraway seeds

+ 1 tbsp juniper berries, crushed

+ 600ml stock – lamb stock is too strong, chicken or veal is best

+ 2 bell peppers, diced

+ 400g waxy potatoes, peeled and diced small

+ Splash of fino sherry

+ Salt and pepper

+ 200ml crème fraiche

What you do

Heat the dripping or oil in a frying pan at medium-high heat. Fry the steaks on both sides for two minutes each to colour them. Remove them and chop into walnut-size pieces. The reason for frying first and chopping afterwards is that the meat remains tender. It can be tough if you chop first and fry later.

Lower heat to medium and cook the onions and garlic till soft, about seven minutes. Add the carrots, celery, peppers, potatoes, and paprika, caraway seeds, and juniper berries. Fry for another ten minutes, then add the stock and the cubed meat. Bring to a gentle bubble and simmer for at least half an hour. Season and add sherry. Simmer for another fifteen minutes.

Taste. The lamb should be meltingly tender. If it's not, simmer for a bit longer.

Serve in bowls with a dollop of crème fraiche in each bowl.

MUSHROOM SOUP FOR A COLD NIGHT

If you value your sanity do not start reading up about mushrooms. They are a most complicated species. And if you value your health don't pop off into the woods to gather some lovely wild mushrooms for supper unless you know exactly what you are doing. Death by eating the wrong mushroom is almost as bad as rabies with your muscles deciding to go to war with each other. No fun at all. This soup, on the other hand, is relaxing and soothing, just the thing for when the wind is howling down your chimney.

Ingredients for four

+ 50g butter

+ 300g button or field mushrooms, chopped small

+ 100g dried chanterelle, morel, and cepes (or just one or two of these)

+ 1 medium onion, chopped fine

+ 1 garlic clove, squashed and chopped

+ 750ml chicken stock

+ 150ml fino sherry

+ 100ml crème fraîche

What you do

Pour enough boiling water over the dried mushrooms to cover them in a bowl or jug. Sauté the onion and garlic over medium heat until softened, about seven minutes. Drain the dried mushrooms, keeping the juice, chop them up, not too small, and add to the pan, cooking for another five minutes.

Add the stock, sherry, and 500ml of reserved juice, bring to the boil, then simmer for 20 mins. Briefly blitz the soup with a stick blender, stopping before you have a puree. Leaving a few chunks and shreds gives a good texture. Stir a blob of crème fraiche into each bowl before serving.

> "If you value your sanity do not start reading up about mushrooms."

SMOKED HADDOCK CHOWDER

Few things are more comforting than smoked haddock chowder. Outside, the winter wind is howling, inside, a fire is roaring. That is haddock chowder time. Although, strangely, it's also good in summer.

I have one request. Don't buy yellow, dyed, smoked haddock. That is like substituting spam for ham in a recipe. Use undyed smoked haddock, pale-fleshed with no suspicious yellow flecks. This is one of the most under-rated and best of sea food, also one of the cheapest.

If you don't feel like making the chowder below, you can follow the first bit of the recipe, simmering the haddock in milk and water long enough so you can easily remove the skin and flake the fish. Then use the flaked fish in scrambled eggs or an omelette. Eggs and smoked fish have a strong affinity. Or don't cook the fish at all but slice it horizontally into paper-thin slices and use it as the basis for your favourite ceviche recipe. Or you can make an Omelette Arnold Bennet, a delicious dish, but too much of a faff for me to make so I recommend that instead you save up and go to the Savoy Grill for it where it was originally served. My ex-wife used to make a spectacular smoked haddock soufflé and, if you are good at soufflés, give that a try. It may have been the fact that I ate the soufflé with ketchup which resulted in our divorce.

Perhaps the simplest and the most universally enjoyed haddock recipe is the chowder below.

Ingredients for eight

+ 600g smoked undyed haddock
+ Big splash of olive oil
+ Big splodge of butter
+ 2 onions, finely chopped
+ 1kg waxy potatoes chopped into small pieces
+ 3 leeks chopped into rounds
+ 350g sweetcorn, frozen is fine
+ 4 slices pancetta or good streaky bacon, diced
+ 1 tbsp fresh thyme or 1 tsp of dried
+ 100ml Pernod
+ 750ml full cream milk
+ 200ml single cream
+ Chopped spring onions, chives, or parsley
+ Salt and pepper

What you do

Bring half the milk and 400ml of water to a low boil in a wok or deep frying pan. Turn down the heat to low and slide in the haddock cut into pieces three or four inches long. Leave for a short ten minutes. Keep the liquid but remove the fish on to a large plate and peel off the skin. Flake the haddock in your hands into tablespoon sized chunks. Reserve on a plate.

Meanwhile put a large saucepan on medium-high heat with the olive oil and butter. Add the potato, onion, and leeks. After two minutes bring heat down to medium and leave the vegetables to soften, giving them an occasional stir.

After another ten minutes turn the heat off and remove half the vegetables to a large bowl, add the reserved cooking liquid and liquidise with a stick blender. Add this back to the pot together with the remaining milk. Add the sweetcorn, bacon, thyme, cream, and Pernod. Season with salt and pepper. Bring to a simmer and leave simmering gently for ten minutes. Add the reserved fish, stir gently, simmer for another five minutes and serve in soup plates with a sprinkling of chopped spring onions, chives or parsley.

BACK LANE WINTER CRAB SOUP

Please have a look at the preamble to **Back Lane Summer Crab Soup** **(see p. 64)** before you go ahead with this recipe. There are some general comments there about crabs that you may find useful. This soup, inspired by wonderful American crab soups, is one of my favourites. You don't have to do much. Let the crabs do the work.

Ingredients for four

+ 1 yellow onion, chopped

+ 1 fennel bulb, cored and chopped, reserving the fennel fronds

+ 2 sticks celery, chopped

+ 1 garlic clove, crushed and sliced

+ 1 tbsp tomato ketchup

+ 1 tbsp olive oil

+ 1 tbsp butter

+ 5 crabs, cooked and picked, mixed brown and white meat

+ 1 tbsp Old Bay Seasoning (the original American crab seasoning, use ½ tbsp of sweet paprika if you don't have it)

+ Good splash of bourbon, use rum if you don't have it

+ 1l crab stock made by boiling up crab shells and the less good meat

+ 100ml double cream

+ 3 thick slices sourdough bread cut into small croutons

+ Salt and pepper

What you do

Put a glug of olive oil and a splodge of butter in a large saucepan, add the onion, fennel, garlic, and celery with a pinch of salt and cook on medium heat until soft, about ten minutes. Stir in the tomato ketchup at the end.

Add the bourbon and Old Bay, the stock, and stir until smooth. Blitz the soup briefly with a stick blender. Don't overdo the blitzing. You are not trying to make a puree; you should still have recognisable chunky bits. Add the brown crabmeat and half the white. Give it a good stir.

Cover with a lid and simmer gently for fifteen minutes.

Add the cream and simmer very gently, don't boil, for another five minutes. Add a few drops of lemon juice, taste and season with pepper and maybe some more salt.

Heat the oven to 200C. While the soup is simmering, toss the croutons with the remaining oil, and some black pepper on a baking tray. Bake for 10 mins, tossing halfway through, until crisp and golden. Leave to cool.

To serve, ladle the soup into bowls. Spoon a mound of white crabmeat into the centre of each bowl, drizzle with a little oil and add the reserved fennel fronds. Float a few croutons on top and serve with a grind of black pepper.

BACK LANE SUMMER CRAB SOUP

Crabs. One of the glories of the English coast. Fresh and sweet. There are many different crab species distributed around the world, spider crabs, mud crabs, Dungeness crabs, and scores more. Naturally everyone knows that their local crab is the best and only one. It's not an argument worth getting into but I can say that the British brown crab, *cancer pagurus*, a modest-looking creature about five inches across, pinky-brown in colour and with a pie-crust edge to its shell, is a fine and wonderful thing, a far more interesting taste than lobster. One of the simplest and best ways to eat it is cold with mayonnaise, a squeeze of lemon and a sliver of buttered brown toast.

It also makes terrific soup. I have two versions, a chilled one for the summer, and a velvety hot one for the winter.

The chilled one is up there with gazpacho and *ajo blanco* at the top of the best ever summer soups list. I borrowed some of the recipe for chilled soup from Nigel Slater but have altered it. His soup tastes like flavoured yogurt. I have added some things to give it an added smoothness and zing. While the summer soup is as English as summer pudding, the winter one, ***Back Lane Winter Crab Soup (see p. 62)***, is transatlantic. The Americans love their crabs. Theirs are different to English crabs but when it comes to crab soup or crab cakes theirs and ours are both delicious. Ours are a touch sweeter and theirs a bit chunkier. My winter crab soup recipe is made up from a variety of excellent crab soups I have had over the years on the eastern seaboard of America.

Two warnings. You must not used tinned crab. No, sorry, but no. It must be fresh. Use tinned crab for something else. Can't think what offhand. Give it to the cat? And, for God's sake, don't even think about using the "crabsticks" you find at English supermarket fish counters. No-one knows what a "crabstick" is made from, some kind of extruded marine matter, but it certainly has nothing to do with a crab.

You don't have to use the British brown crab. If you live on Chesapeake Bay or in Sydney or Marseille, feel free to substitute one of your excellent local crabs. Me, I'll stick with Norfolk browns. You can buy whole crabs, boil them, and take them apart yourself but it's hard work discarding the lungs and lining and other bits you don't want and picking out the bits you do. I buy mine ready cooked and dressed from my excellent local fishmonger whose crabs were caught yesterday, possibly today. If you're lucky you have a fishmonger who will sell you sparklingly fresh, dressed crabs. If not you better get the pliers out and set to work.

"There are many different crab species distributed around the world, spider crabs, mud crabs, Dungeness crabs, and scores more. Naturally everyone knows that their local crab is the best and only one."

Ingredients for four

+ 1 large cucumber
+ 1 tsp sea salt
+ 1 clove garlic
+ 500ml Greek yogurt
+ ½ tsp chilli flakes
+ 1 tbsp wine vinegar
+ Small bunch of mint (to give about 4 tbsp chopped leaves)
+ 100ml single cream
+ 100ml fino sherry (or dry vermouth)
+ 100ml full cream milk
+ 1 small red bell pepper, very finely chopped
+ 4 dressed crabs

What you do

Peel the cucumber, halve it, scrape out the seeds with a teaspoon then chop into tiny bits. Tip the cucumber into a colander, sprinkle with a teaspoonful of salt, give it a shake and leave it in the sink to drain for a good half hour.

Peel and crush the garlic and add to the yogurt in a bowl. Mix chilli flakes into the yogurt with the vinegar. Remove the leaves from the mint and chop them finely, then stir the chopped mint into the mixture.

Stir in the cucumber, but not the liquid that has drained from it, and then the cream, sherry, and milk. Give the mixture a quick blitz with a stick blender.

Scrape out the insides of the dressed crabs and add them to the mixture, all the brown meat and half the white. Give everything a good stir. Season with black pepper and chill in the fridge. It must be really cold if it is to be good.

Divide the soup between four bowls. Put a spoon of the reserved white meat in the middle of each bowl, sprinkle the finely chopped red pepper on top and serve before it gets warm.

CLAUDIA'S LOBSTER HOTPOT

I have supported Reprieve for many years. They are an admirable charity fighting against capital punishment and torture in places like Pakistan, Saudi Arabia, and the United States. They represented the British detainees at Guantanamo Bay.

At their annual dinner in 2018 I bid on and won one of the prizes, a dinner for four cooked by Claudia Roden in her own kitchen. You know who Claudia is, an amazing woman of Jewish-Egyptian descent who moved to England and has written some of the best cook books on Middle Eastern and Mediterranean cooking. She is even better than her books. Four of us went to her Arts and Crafts house in Hampstead where we sat in wonder in her kitchen while she busied around cooking us the best *meze* dinner we had ever eaten.

I particularly love her *The Food of Spain* book because I particularly love Spanish food. This recipe and the Crab in Cider recipe were inspired by recipes in that book with a few tweaks of mine.

The Lobster Hotpot or Caldareta de Langosta, says Claudia, is a Menorcan recipe. To make the dish more affordable she adds some firm fish like monkfish, which costs less than lobster, or langouste if you are in the Mediterranean. I've used lobster only – I can get them relatively cheaply in Norfolk – but feel free to substitute some firm fish for some of the lobster if you want to keep the cost down.

She uses fish stock. That's good if you've got it or want to make it. I cheat. For me there is no better base for a fish soup than brown crabmeat. Sometimes I add the crabmeat direct to the soup. For this recipe, I buy the wonderful Soupe de Crabe from Le Touquet available in bottles from any good deli or fishmonger, and add that instead. It is a rich brown colour, thick with brown crab meat. It's a terrific fish soup base.

Ingredients for six

+ 2 medium onions, peeled and chopped

+ 3 tablespoons olive oil

+ 350g truly ripe tomatoes, peeled and chopped; if they are not properly ripe, use tinned tomatoes

+ 1 teaspoon sugar (not needed if the tomatoes are sweet)

+ 1l fish stock or Soupe de Crabe (see text above)

+ 125ml brandy

+ 50ml Pernod

+ 2 tsp chilli flakes

+ Salt and pepper

+ 2 tsp ground fennel seeds

+ 2 handfuls of clams or cockles, not mussels

+ 3 1kg cooked lobsters, halved down the middle, heads removed and discarded, claws well cracked (most fishmongers' lobsters are much smaller, about 500g; these have a lot of shell and not much flesh so try to order decent-sized lobsters in advance)

For the picada

+ 100g almond flakes

+ 3 garlic cloves, peeled

+ 1 tbsp white wine or sherry vinegar (not balsamic)

+ 1 tbsp olive oil

+ 1 handful of flat-leaf parsley, coarsely chopped

+ 4 tablespoons brandy

What you do

In a deep Le Creuset casserole or equivalent, fry the onion in the oil over a low heat until very soft. Add the tomatoes and cook over medium heat until the sauce is reduced and jammy. Taste and add sugar if the tomatoes are acid. Add the fish stock or Soupe de Crabe, the chilli flakes, the ground fennel seeds, and the brandy and Pernod. Season with salt and pepper. Take a stick blender and whir to a thick consistency.

Meanwhile, for the *picada*, brown the almonds and garlic in a dry frying pan. Take them out and pound them to a paste with the chopped parsley and vinegar in a mortar. Put the oil in the pan and add the paste together with the brandy, mix well over a medium heat and then add to the soup.

Turn the heat to medium high and add the clams. When they are open, about three minutes, turn the heat down to medium and add the cooked lobster. Stir everything well to make sure the lobster is well coated in sauce.

Dish this out in bowls together with some toasted slices of good country bread for dunking.

SWEDISH FISH SOUP

I could live on fish soup. In this book fish soup recipes are divided roughly into two categories. There is the Mediterranean type, based on onions, tomatoes and garlic, and the northern ones which are thick and creamy of which **Smoked Haddock Chowder (see p. 61)** and my **Back Lane Summer and Winter crab soups (see p. 64 and 62)** are a good example. Of course, there are many other types of fish soup, particularly the Asian ones; think Thai and Vietnamese, for instance, but you can find out about those from someone more knowledgeable than I about Asian cooking.

This is a Swedish recipe . These days Scandinavia has a wonderful new cuisine based on fresh ingredients and foraged food. This is not one of those. This is an old fashioned, fill you up, traditional soup, the kind of thing the Scandinavians have been eating on long summer nights and dark chilly evenings for centuries. I can't remember where this recipe was foraged from. I've been cooking it for years and I expect it's changed over that time. Like all my fish soups it is not something to be served in a small cup as a starter. This soup is a meal in itself.

Ingredients for four

+ 1 large onion, chopped

+ 1 stick celery, chopped

+ ½ fennel bulb, chopped

+ 750ml fish stock (if you don't have fish stock, please do not use a stock cube, aka salt bomb, use vegetable or chicken stock)

+ 4 cloves garlic, chopped

+ 400g canned chopped tomatoes

+ 200ml dry white vermouth, or dry white wine

+ 500g new potatoes, quartered

+ 1 tsp nutmeg

+ 2 tsp ground fennel seeds

+ 300g firm white fish, haddock and halibut are my favourites but you could use hake or cod, cut into bite-sized chunks

+ Big handful of fresh cockles or clams, mussels if you can't get them

+ 300g peeled medium-sized prawns, frozen if you must

+ 100ml double cream

+ 2 tbsp fresh dill, chopped

+ 3 tbsp crème fraiche

+ Butter

+ Olive oil

+ Salt and pepper

What you do

Put a good splodge of butter in a big saucepan on medium heat. Add the onion, celery, potatoes, fennel, and garlic and cook gently until they are soft, probably fifteen minutes.

Add the tomatoes, vermouth, and stock, cook for two minutes to assimilate the tomatoes, and then add nutmeg and fennel seeds and simmer for about ten minutes.

Add the fish, shrimps, and cockles. Add salt and pepper and taste for seasoning. Turn the heat up to medium-high as the fish will have cooled down the mixture. Cook for five minutes. Check that the cockles have opened, check seasoning again, lower heat to low, and stir in the cream.

Put the soup in bowls, sprinkle some dill on the top, add a spoonful of crème fraiche in the middle, and serve. Some toasted sourdough bread for dunking is a good idea.

MILO'S GOA-NORFOLK FISH SOUP

I have a lot of favourite recipes but this is one that I get asked for most often. If you want a genuine Goan curry, you can find lots of excellent recipes. However, Goa, blessed as it is with so many wonderful ingredients, coconuts, mangoes, and spices, lacks one thing we have in chilly England – North Sea and English Channel fish and shellfish. Goa has the pomfret, a nice enough fish; England has turbot, brill, halibut, sole… Sorry pomfret, you lose, it's no contest. If the Goans were lucky enough to have our fish, they wouldn't use pomfret either. Many fruits, vegetables, fish and meat taste better if they are raised in cooler northern climes where growing

and ripening takes longer than in the sweaty regions. Few things match a white English peach, or a French mirabelle plum, Scottish beef, Swiss mountain cheese, or North Sea fish. Try comparing a tropical Caribbean lobster with one from Maine's chilly waters. Again, no contest.

This recipe also uses an ingredient little used in Indian cooking outside Goa, vinegar, one of the many legacies of its erstwhile Portuguese rulers. We Brits never ruled Goa but it didn't stop us stealing their best cooks. Any *pukka sahib* in British India who liked food would do his best to lay hands on a Goan chef.

My Goan fish soup has some special English ingredients in it. My key add to the recipe is an English brown crab. If the Goans had our crabs I am convinced they would join me in heaping it into their fish soups.

I say it elsewhere but let's say it again here. If you are lucky enough to live in England and you want to make a fish soup, then adding the brown meat from a British crab will give your sauce a depth, suavity, and texture that nothing else can match.

Ingredients for four

For the *masala*

+ 1 tsp cloves*
+ 1 tbsp coriander seeds*
+ 1 tbsp cumin seeds*
+ 1 tbsp mustard seeds*
+ 1 tbsp turmeric*
+ 1 tsp allspice*

Everything else

+ 1 tbsp light brown sugar
+ 1 tsp salt
+ 4 garlic cloves, peeled, crushed, and chopped
+ 4 3-inch chopped chillies (de-seed and cut out the pith if you don't like it too hot; if you want to use ground chilli flakes instead, go ahead but your soup won't have the same freshness)
+ 2 inches root ginger, peeled and chopped small
+ 1 tbsp white vinegar
+ 3 tbsp vegetable oil
+ 2 small or one large onion, finely chopped
+ 400ml tin of coconut milk
+ 200ml yoghurt
+ 100ml cachaça or white rum (the nearest you can get to Goan palm toddy)
+ 3 dressed brown crabs with brown and white meat separated
+ 400g firm white not-oily fish, I use halibut, or haddock cut into bite-size chunks
+ 200g prawns, fresh whole prawns are best if you can get them. Leave them whole and people can peel and eat them in their fingers.

If you don't have them use big frozen raw ones. Thaw in advance and discard the liquid.

+ 10 mussels, clams, or cockles
+ Bunch of coriander chopped

What you do

Heat a big, deep frying pan or wok, to medium high. Put in all the masala spices, the ones with an asterisk above, and toast them till they smoke and release fragrance, about three minutes. Take them out and pound them to near-powder in a mortar or whir them in a blender.

Heat 3 tbsp oil in the pan over a medium heat, then add the onion, garlic, ginger and chopped chillies. Fry until the onions are soft but not brown, about five to seven minutes. Add the pounded masala mix. Mix well and fry for a couple of minutes more.

Add the coconut milk, vinegar, yoghurt, cachaça, and 200ml water. Bring to the boil, then turn down the heat and simmer for about ten minutes until the sauce has thickened slightly. Add sugar, salt and pepper and taste. Put the brown meat from the crabs in a bowl. Add a few ladles of the soup to the bowl and stir the brown meat till it blends without lumps into the liquid. Add this to the soup. Stir to mix well. Bring to a gentle boil and add the rest of the seafood. Cook for about five minutes on medium-high heat when the fish should be cooked through. Remember the fish will go on cooking after the heat is turned off.

Serve in bowls with green coriander chopped over the top. I don't add rice. This is a meal in itself just as much as a Mediterranean fish soup, it's not a sauce for rice.

ZING-A-LING FISH SOUP

Everywhere in the world has a fish soup: first among equals, bouillabaisse, and don't get me started on what goes into *le vrai bouillabaisse*, it's worse than arguing in Castelnaudary over *le vrai cassoulet*; San Francisco's delicious cioppino, the day's catch stewed up with tomato and herbs; bourride from Nice, just that little bit posher than its Marseillaise cousin, bouillabaisse; chowders, I could write a book on chowders; the hundred varieties of Spanish sopa marinera with a hundred different names; tom yum from Thailand; the Greek psarosoupas, each island with its different recipe; cullen skink from Scotland; and all kinds of coconutty marvels from South India and Sri Lanka. I love them all.

They have one thing in common, a strong sense of place.

Everyone loves my Sicilian fish soup. It should be made with Mediterranean fish. The ingredients are local to Sicily even if the Pernod comes from Marseilles. The soup's unique feature which I can't find in any other recipe comes from something I was told by a friend who loves to eat and who has been sailing the Mediterranean longer than Odysseus. "Miles," he said, "Try this when you next make a fish soup; they do it in Palermo. They soak stale bread in vinegar, add toasted almonds and then pound it all up to the consistency of polenta. This they add to the soup. The bread and almonds give body to the soup and the vinegar gives it freshness and zing but for God's sake don't overdo the vinegar. It's kind of Arab, sweet-sour."

So here it is. The perfect Mediterranean dinner dish for eight people, or, if you have a big pot, double the ingredients and feed sixteen. With a zing.

Ingredients for eight

For the prawn stock

+ Prawn heads (from prawns, below)

+ 1 chopped carrot

+ 1 onion peeled and quartered

+ 1 stick of celery chopped

For the soup

+ 500g large raw prawns in their shells

+ 2 onions, finely chopped

+ 2 sticks celery, finely chopped

+ 3 garlic cloves, finely chopped

+ 3 400g tins of chopped tomatoes

+ 400ml prawn stock, though you can use previously made fish or chicken stock if you're feeling lazy

+ 200ml vermouth / fino sherry / white wine, in order of preference

+ 50ml Pernod

+ 1kg firm Mediterranean fish chopped into inch cubes (swordfish is best, monkfish is good, tuna – OK but a bit oily; I don't use whole fish like sea bass, sea bream or rouget because they disintegrate too easily and separating bone and skin from fish is too much of a labour; if you have to use a non-Mediterranean fish go for halibut, haddock or cod).

+ 500g fresh in-the-shell cockles or clams (use mussels if you can't get cockles or clams)

+ 3 medium squid, chopped into rounds

+ (Optional but essential if you live in Norfolk) 3 dressed Norfolk crabs

+ 2 tsp chilli flakes

+ 2 tsp dried thyme

+ 2 tsp fennel seed

+ Handful of flat parsley

+ 3 slices stale bread

+ 3 tbsp wine vinegar

+ Handful almond flakes

+ Salt and pepper

What you do

Break off the prawns' heads and put them in a saucepan with a splash of olive oil over medium heat. Add carrot, celery, and onion. Squash the heads with a wooden spatula. After a couple of minutes, add enough water to cover the solids by a couple of inches. Bring to the boil and simmer for thirty minutes. Strain into a bowl.

Take a big saucepan, add oil, onions, garlic, and celery. Let them soften over medium heat, then add the chopped tomatoes, stock, vermouth/sherry/wine, Pernod, chilli flakes, thyme, and fennel seeds. Bring to a boil, stir, and then taste. Should be spicy but not hot. If the tomatoes are acid add a teaspoon of sugar. Reduce a bit, then put lid on and leave to stew on gentle heat for half an hour.

Meanwhile you will have torn up the bread and put it in a bowl to soak with the vinegar. Toast the almond flakes until they brown and add them to the bowl. Add this mixture to a blender with enough ladles of soup to make it blendable. Give it a whir until the mixture becomes the consistency of polenta. Put on one side.

Taste the soup mixture. Add salt and pepper to taste. Spoon a couple more ladles of soup into the bread mixture to make it liquid enough to pour. Gradually add this to the soup, stirring as you go so the mixture spreads evenly and does not clump up. Taste. Should have a fresh zing from the vinegar without tasting vinegary.

The next step is optional. It's not Mediterranean but adding the crabs does make your soup taste wonderfully suave and deep. Spoon out the dark and white meat from the crabs into a bowl. Add a couple of ladles of the soup, stir the crabmeat around to blend it with the soup and add back to the soup saucepan.

Turn heat up to a vigorous bubble and add the fish and shellfish. Lower heat to a gentle bubble, put a lid on and go back to eating your first course. After a short ten minutes the fish will be cooked. Either serve from the cooking pot or pour into a warmed earthenware bowl.

Ladle out into bowls with a sprinkle of chopped flat parsley on top.

Lightly toasted sourdough bread slices go well with this for dunking.

CATAPLANA

Cataplana is a new favourite which, as a newcomer to Portugal, I discovered recently when I was dodging Covid lockdown in Vila Real de Santo Antonio, a town of cobbled streets and graceful squares on the south coast of Portugal, looking across the River Guadiana into Spain. The cataplana itself is a cooking vessel. It is to a Portuguese cook what a wok is to a Chinese or a paella pan to a Valencian. Traditionally made from copper, it is often in these days of induction cooking made from steel as copper won't work on an induction hob. The cataplana is shaped like a giant clamshell, a foot or more across, with each half being about six inches deep and with catches round the sides to keep it tightly closed. In the Algarve they cook lots of things in their cataplanas, not just fish; they often mix meat, always pork or pork sausage, with the fish. The ingredients for a traditional cataplana are, like so many fishermen's dishes, whatever you have to hand that day. Cooking fish stews is not like baking where you have to get the proportions and temperatures right. Fish stews are generous and forgiving. Do what you want and add what you like as long as you obey the cardinal rule: don't overcook the fish.

Nearly all cataplanas have onions, peppers, and garlic. Most have chorizo and bacon. Many have potatoes and just about all of them have fish and shellfish. There are exceptions but you can look those up in a Portuguese cookbook if you're curious.

This recipe below invariably gets greedily finished up. Feel free to modify the recipe to suit what you have but avoid oily fish like salmon and mackerel.

Ingredients for four

+ 2 tbsp olive oil

+ 100g lardons

+ 100g chorizo chopped into half-moons

+ 1 large onion sliced into half-moons

+ 1 green or red pepper chopped

+ 200g potato sliced into half-moons the thickness of a pound coin

+ 2 x 400g cans chopped tomatoes

+ 4 cloves garlic chopped

+ 1 tsp chilli flakes

+ 250ml dry sherry or dry white vermouth

+ 100ml cachaca or white rum

+ 400g firm white fish chopped into inch-square chunks

+ 8 medium-sized prawns in their shells

+ 1 handful mussels

+ 2 handfuls clams

+ 1 small squid, cleaned and sliced into rounds

+ Salt and pepper

+ Parsley

What you do

Heat the oil in the cataplana, or, if you don't have a cataplana, a thick-bottomed lidded casserole, and add the lardons and chorizo. Cook at medium heat, stirring, for five minutes and then remove and reserve. Add onions, peppers, garlic and potatoes and let them cook on medium heat, picking up the colour from the chorizo oil, for a short ten minutes with the occasional stir.

Add the tomatoes, sherry/ vermouth, cachaca/rum, chilli flakes, salt and pepper. Reduce to a simmer and cook with the lid off for 15 minutes. Taste and adjust seasoning if necessary.

Add back the lardons and chorizo, give it a good stir, and cook over low heat for 15 minutes with the lid on. Having done this you can relax. Leave the cataplana in a quiet corner until you are ready to sit down to dinner. Just before you sit down for the first course, put the cataplana on high heat and when it starts to bubble add the fish and shellfish. Turn the heat down to a simmer and replace the lid. Let it cook for ten minutes and then turn the heat off and let it sit till you have finished your first course.

Open the lid, sprinkle some chopped parsley or coriander over the stew. Serve in deep bowls with more bowls in the middle of the table for the empty shells. Toasted sourdough is good for dunking.

Fishy

BRILL BRILL

This is my go-to Christmas Eve dish but it's far too good to eat only on Christmas Eve. My Christmas Eve menu is simple. Start with caviar. I know no-one can afford it but I can because the government sends me £200 just before Christmas every year as my "winter fuel allowance". I know no finer winter fuel than caviar so I shoot off to my Iranian man the far end of Kensington High Street where there are two "competing" Iranian shops both actually owned by the same honest Iranian. In exchange for £200 he sells me what he assures me is finest Iranian wild caviar. What he doesn't know is that I know the code. Every tin of caviar has some letters on the bottom which tell you what type of sturgeon it comes from and the country of origin. So when he says genuine Iranian I turn the tin over and read BAE/C/DE/2021/PO5/VH100 on the bottom. BAE is the type of fish, in this case the Acipenser Baerii, a type of sturgeon. C means cultivated as opposed to W, wild. DE means Germany, the country

of production. 2021 is the year of harvest and the rest of the letters identify the batch and processing number. Any caviar you buy legally in London is farmed. If they say it is wild Caspian caviar they are either lying or Mr Abramovich. But it's fun to know the code and catch them selling you Chinese farmed caviar as Caspian Special. Nothing wrong with the Chinese stuff. Or the French, Belgian, American, even Devon caviar. They're delicious and they are what you will buy in Kaspia in Paris or London. Or in my Iranian shops. Visit attiluscaviar.co.uk/pages/certification if you want to know the code.

Caviar for starter is followed by Brill Brill for the main course and then *Dad's Mango Kulfi (p.156)* for dessert. I've passed the ritual of making Dad's Mango Kulfi on to Tasha who, I'm sorry to say, makes it better than I do.

Brill is one the finest fish in the sea, although, like the caviar, most of it is farmed. I have nothing against farmed fish. If it's done in clean

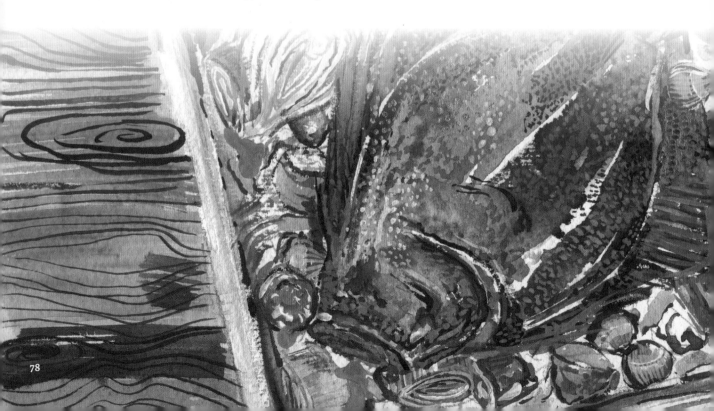

conditions it's a lot better than no fish. Brill and Turbot (which is similar to Brill but even better and more expensive; it can easily be substituted in this recipe), like most expensive fish, such as Dover Sole, do not need to be fresh out of the sea. A few days in the fridge brings out the taste. It's the cheap but delicious fish like mackerel, plaice, and lemon sole which need to be really fresh or they turn to mush when you cook them.

And, please, don't buy brill fillets from the fishmonger. Cooking a fish on the bone makes it taste so much better because, as with a chicken, the real flavour is in the bones. That's why you use them to make stock.

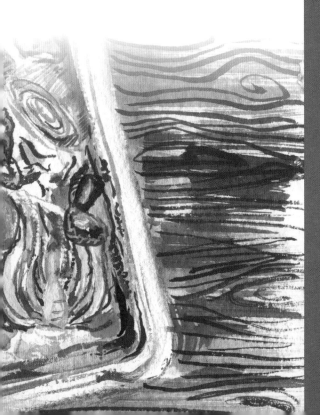

Ingredients for four

+ 1 Brill, or Turbot, about a foot long from nose to tail, say, 1.5kg
+ Butter
+ Olive oil
+ 6 waxy new potatoes
+ Fennel bulb, diced fine
+ 2 leeks, chopped
+ 4 carrots, chopped
+ 1 onion, roughly chopped
+ 500ml white wine / fino sherry / white vermouth
+ Dash of Pernod
+ Salt and pepper

What you do

Take a round lidded casserole, the shallow 30cm Le Creuset one is good, put it on medium heat and add a good blob of butter and an equivalent splodge of olive oil. Chop up the potatoes, fennel, and carrots into half-inch chunks, cut the leek into rounds, and roughly chop the onion. Put them all in the pan, put the lid on, and give it a stir every few minutes.

Turn the oven on to 200c.

When the vegetables start to soften, about ten minutes, take the pan off the heat. Add salt and pepper. Splash in the 500ml of wine/sherry/ vermouth. Any of these or a mixture is good. I like all three. Finish it off with a glug of Pernod if you have some.

Pernod and fish go together like Beyoncé and tight jeans.

Put the fish on top, dark skin side up. You may have to chop off the head and tail to make it fit in the pan. That's fine. I also trim the outer layer of bone from the edge of the fish.

Put the lid on the pan and pop it in the oven. (You can always cook this on a medium hob if you don't want to use your oven.)

Take it out after fifteen minutes and test. If the skin comes away easily it is cooked. If not put it back for another five minutes and test again until the skin comes away easily.

Take the fish out of the pan on to a big chopping board. Remove skin completely and take the flesh off in strips an inch or so wide. Flip the fish and remove the whitish skin from the underside. Slice in the same way.

Scoop the vegetable mixture into soup bowls, top with slices of brill and spoon the liquid over the fish and vegetables, give it a grind of pepper and salt, serve.

Feel free to chop some chives or parsley over the dish and feel free to add some cream to the liquid. I don't because I like the clean taste of the pure stock.

HOLY HALIBUT!

So highly prized was the halibut that it was called the Holy Fish, its name coming from the Old English Haly, or holy, and Butte, flat fish. It was the monk's favourite when Friday came round. It was probably only the monks who could afford to eat it as it has always been expensive. You can find halibut in the Mediterranean, its wonderful Italian name being Ippoglosso, but it's really a fish that thrives in the deep, cold waters of the northern Atlantic between Norway and Greenland. The biggest halibut ever caught was in Norwegian waters. It was more than twice the weight of Boris Johnson and almost nine feet long.

Halibut, dover sole, and turbot are the aristocrats of English fish cookery. They are also frighteningly expensive. Are they worth it? You can ask the same thing about ribeye or fillet steak. You are not going to eat these every day but a dinner with halibut or dover sole for two

people at home will still cost you a lot less than dinner for two at Sheekey's or The Ivy. Go on, spoil yourself. And I don't mean go to Sheekey's.

Fish, more than meat, is a matter of personal taste. I don't like cod (see ***Salmon for Supper (p. 86)*** for why), Lots of other people love it. I'm not keen on monkfish despite the fact people tell you it tastes "just like lobster". It doesn't, and it has a strange, for a fish, chewy texture. Not for me, but you go right ahead.

I was curious what different fish cost so, in 2021, I checked out the Waitrose website to see what they were selling fish fillets for. Not all fish is sold filleted. Dover sole is nearly always sold whole, as are mackerel and herring. There's a lot of skin and bone on a Dover sole. Only a third of the weight is left when you've got rid of that. Waitrose don't sell turbot but it's usually much the same price as Dover sole.

The table below is not in price order but in order of how much I like the fish. Feel free to re-order the table in line with your own taste. The price per kilo is in brackets after the fish. I've adjusted things like dover sole which are sold whole to give a price for the edible part only.

1. Dover sole (£75) and turbot (£75)
2. Halibut (£47)
3. Haddock (£20) and undyed smoked haddock (£17)
4. Sea bass (£32) and sea bream (£30) – both of these are much better on the bone and whole than filleted.
5. Salmon (£18)
6. Hake (£22)
7. Lemon sole (£30)
8. Albacore tuna (£32) and yellowfin tuna (£25)
9. Cod (£21) and monkfish (£40)
10. Trout (£23) and plaice (£13)

> "The biggest halibut ever caught was in Norwegian waters. It was more than twice the weight of Boris Johnson and almost nine feet long."

Here's something else about fish. Generally the less expensive it is, the fresher it needs to be. Dover sole and turbot are better when they are three or four days out of the sea. Cheap fish like plaice, mackerel, herring and flounder must be sparkling fresh or they are disgusting.

For comparison's sake, here are the prices per kilo of upmarket steaks from Waitrose: Wagyu (£69), fillet (£40), sirloin (£30), ribeye (£30), and rump (£20), surprisingly similar to the fish prices.

Here's a good way to cook halibut. A problem with fish cookery is that fish needs little cooking, usually no more than a few minutes. Overcooked fish goes mushy and is fit only for the bin. Vegetables to go with the fish need longer cooking. What I've done here is cook them separately and then combine them towards the end.

Ingredients for two

+ Two halibut steaks, 150g to 200g each
+ 6 fresh shell-on prawns (if you only have frozen, forget it)
+ 1 medium onion, sliced thin
+ 8 button mushrooms, sliced
+ 150g peas, frozen are fine
+ 1 clove of garlic, chopped
+ Thumb of ginger, chopped small
+ 250ml dry white vermouth or wine
+ Olive oil
+ Butter
+ Salt and pepper

What you do

Take a big frying pan and cook the onions, garlic, and ginger with oil and butter over medium heat till they are soft but not brown. I put a lid on for part of the time to speed the process up.

Take another frying pan with a thick base and a good lid and put over medium-high heat. Add oil and a butter. Pat the halibut steaks dry with a paper towel and put in the pan. The idea is to lightly brown the fish on both sides, maybe 90 seconds per side, then take them out and put them on a plate.

Turn the heat down to medium and add the by-now-soft onion mixture, followed by the mushrooms and peas. Put the halibut back on top of the vegetables, pour over the vermouth, add the prawns, season with salt and pepper, put a lid on the pan and cook for between five and ten minutes. How long it takes will depend on the thickness of your steaks. You can test by probing into the middle, next to the bone, with a sharp knife. If the flesh is translucent, it needs a bit more cooking but if it's white all through, take it off immediately.

This dish may sound bland, but with things as good and pure as North Sea halibut, anything you add will only detract from the exquisite taste of fresh halibut.

Serve in soup plates. Put the halibut in first, spoon vegetable mixture over it and divide the sauce between the plates. I put a knob of butter on top of each steak.

SEA BREAM AND COCKLES

I love sea bream with its firm, sweet flesh. Same for sea bass, which would be equally good in this recipé. It's hard to say which is better and, although they are not related, in cooking they are pretty much interchangeable. Be careful though because both are easily ruined by over-cooking. Give either three minutes too long and their firm white flesh has turned to mush.

Now that we travel around so much it's useful to know what these fish are called when they pop up on European menus. In France sea bream of the type we most often eat, gilt-head bream in English, is *dorade* or *daurade* in French, keeping up the gold connection. That gets shortened to *orata* or *orada* as you move to Italy and the Adriatic, and *dourada* in Spain and Portugal. You might also like to know that this excellent fish is, like Donald Trump, a member of the *moronidae* family.

Sea bass has many confusing continental aliases because in France, Italy, and Spain it has one name in the North of the country and another in the South. In France sea bass is *bar* in the Atlantic and *loup* or *loup de mer* (it does look a bit predatory and wolfy) in the Mediterranean. In Italy it is *branzino* in the North and *spigola* in the South. They call it something different in Tuscany but I can't remember what. In Spain

they also follow the two-name habit. It's either *lubina* or *mero* although, strictly speaking, *mero* is sea bass's cousin the grouper. So that's all clear?

And don't get me started on what these things are called in America. In the US anything that isn't lobster is identified as snapper. Simple really.

Unless you are in Chile. The Chileans catch a fish almost as ugly as the monkfish. Monkfish is always sold as fillets because the sight of a whole monkfish is deeply disconcerting. It has a head broader than its body and resembles a giant Louis Armstrong with his teeth-sharpened smile. Who wants their dinner grinning at them? The Chileans catch a thing called the Patagonian Tooth Fish in deep Pacific waters. The real sea bass is a shallow water fish. They are always catching them in the surf of my local Norfolk beach. Sea bass are also elegant and well-dressed while the Patagonian Tooth Fish is a marine version of a Chelsea fan. They're so ugly they couldn't sell them until some bright Chilean began exporting them in frozen filleted form to restaurants all over the world as Chilean Sea Bass. You've eaten them in posh restaurants. Nothing to do with sea bass but they taste surprisingly, er, toothsome.

"Farmed fish may not have as much flavour as a wild fish but are more likely to be fresh. I, and you, eat farmed chicken, beef, pork and lamb and as long as they have been raised in good conditions not some awful concentration camp, they taste delicious. Same with sea bass and sea bream."

It's nice to think of sea bream or sea bass swimming around in the North Sea or the Atlantic until some clever fisherman hooks them on a line and a day later they are on your plate. It is nice but it's unlikely to happen. Your sea bream was farmed in Greece and your sea bass in Italy. Or the other way round. Or Turkey. They are the equivalent of Kenyan green beans, efficiently farmed, chilled but not frozen, and popped on a plane that night to London. They are much more likely to be fresh than fish which were caught wild in the North Sea and spent five days on a trawler before being landed.

I've nothing against most farmed fish. They may not have as much flavour as a wild fish but are more likely to be fresh. I, and you, eat farmed chicken, beef, pork and lamb and as long as they have been raised in good conditions not some awful concentration camp, they taste delicious. Same with sea bass and sea bream.

Here's a way to cook sea bream, or sea bass, that I love. It's similar to the **Brill Brill (p.78)** recipe although this is done on the stove top, not in the oven.

Ingredients for two greedy people, or four normal ones

+ 1 sea bream - or sea bass - a foot long, gutted and scaled
+ Two handfuls of in-the-shell cockles or clams (must be fresh and in the shell)
+ Handful of peeled brown shrimps, if you can get them
+ 500ml of white wine, dry white vermouth, or fino sherry
+ Glug of Pernod
+ 2 leeks, chopped into rounds
+ 4 carrots chopped into small pieces
+ 2 cloves garlic, squashed and chopped
+ 1 onion diced
+ 1 fennel bulb diced
+ Salt and pepper

What you do

Put a heavy round Le Creuset cast-iron dish, or your equivalent, on medium high heat, pour in a glug of olive oil and all the vegetables. Sauté them until they are starting to soften, then pour in the wine and Pernod, and lower the heat to medium. Season with salt and pepper.

Put your sea bream on top of this. You may have to cut off the head and tail to fit it in the pan. Put on the lid. Have a look to make sure that the liquid is bubbling but not boiling furiously. The bottom of the fish will be in the liquid, the top will cook by steaming.

After ten minutes lift the lid and make a short lengthwise incision along the backbone. Test gently to see if the flesh comes away from the bone. As soon as it does, take the fish out immediately and put it on a board to carve. Meanwhile throw your cockles and shrimp into the pan, turn the heat up high, pop the lid on and cook for three minutes by which time the cockles will have opened and released their delicious juices into the sauce. Take off the stove. Add a splosh of cream if you must. I don't.

Carve the fish into four long fillets starting with the one along the backbone. Flip and carve the other side. Ladle the vegetables, cockles, and shrimp into soup plates, arrange the fillets on top, spoon lots of broth over the fish, sprinkle with chopped chives or spring onions, and serve with crusty bread and a spoon for drinking the delicious soup.

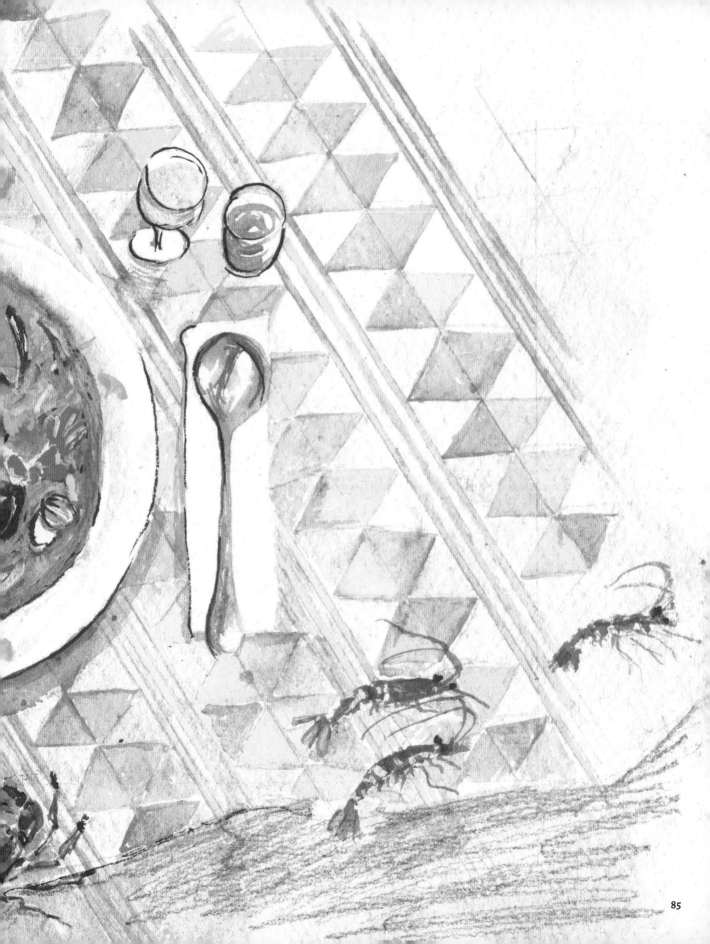

SALMON FOR SUPPER

What a journey fish has come over the last fifty years. I had my first taste of salmon, smoked salmon it was, when I was about ten in the 1950s. It was an almost unimaginable luxury and I was only allowed a couple of bites. If you had not caught the salmon yourself, buying a side of smoked salmon in a shop cost more than the average weekly wage. I pretended to like the salmon but was glad no-one offered me a third bite of this strange textured and coloured beast.

Meanwhile, when I was sent off to a tough naval boarding school aged 8, as was traditional for English children whose parents lived in far-off countries, we were fed twice a week on the cheapest protein available, cod. Cod cost virtually nothing. The North Sea and the Atlantic teemed with it. And when the Stubbington House cook had finished with it, it was one of the most disgusting things on earth, slimy, mushy, fishy in smell, and usually surrounded by a puddle of greenish liquid. People love cod today. I can't eat it.

Today cod is more expensive than ribeye and salmon is as cheap as chicken. People who happily eat farmed chicken, farmed beef, farmed lamb, and farmed pork, get snooty about farmed salmon. Farmed salmon is no different to other farmed table protein. If it's reared in decent surroundings, fed properly, and given enough space by considerate farmers, it is terrific. The same applies to chicken and beef.

Yes, farmed salmon does not taste the same as wild salmon. It has more fat because, like farmed beef, it has led a lazy existence and has not had to do acrobatics swimming up waterfalls to get its rocks off. But I like my beef with some fat on it and I also like the fatty succulence of a well-farmed salmon. If you want to eat wild salmon from the seas around our coasts, dream

on. You can't. A minuscule number of salmon are caught every year in Scottish and Irish rivers but the catch is so small and irregular that none will be offered publicly for sale. The Atlantic salmon, what we like to think of as "true" salmon, is the majestic, hawk-billed, *Salmo salmar*, the king of fish.

You will sometimes see "wild salmon" offered for sale in your supermarket. Yup, it is wild, but it's not the noble *Salmo salmar* of the Atlantic. It could be one of five members of the salmon family with names like Coho, sockeye, chinook, and chum. They are Pacific salmon and they have probably been caught off British Columbia or Alaska. My nephew James, who has sailed the Inside Passage from Vancouver to Juneau, tells me that in places the salmon are so thick in the water you can all but walk on them. James is prone to exaggeration so we can take that with a pinch of salt but the wild, Pacific, salmon is in no danger of dying out. The problem is that it doesn't taste as good as our *Salmo*. It is denser, redder in colour, and less succulent, a coarser eat. It's not bad but I'll stick to Scottish farmed salmon and so should you, but read the label before you buy it. I don't normally put much store by the word organic on a label but I do when it comes to farmed salmon.

Salmon is the easiest thing to cook. I sometimes make a teriyaki-style sauce in which to marinate it and then I grill it and pour the marinade, well-reduced, over it to give you "blackened salmon" as you might have "blackened cod" in Nobu. It's good but below is my simplest go-to recipe for a delicious salmon supper.

"If you want to eat wild salmon from the seas around our coasts, dream on. You can't."

Ingredients for two

+ Two 150g salmon fillets, skin on (I like to eat the skin; you don't have to, but it tastes better if it's cooked with the skin on)

+ 1 medium onion, sliced into strips

+ 1 thumb of ginger, diced

+ 2 cloves of garlic, chopped

+ 6 new potatoes, sliced into coins

+ 1 handful of broad beans or peas (broad beans are best if they are tiny and newly-picked, failing that use frozen petits pois)

+ 4 spring onions chopped

+ 150ml dry white vermouth (Noilly Prat is best), or a dry and fruity white wine

+ Glug of olive oil

+ Splodge of butter

+ Salt and pepper

What you do

Heat a lidded frying-pan on medium heat. Add olive oil and then the vegetables in the order in which they appear above, leaving a gap of a few minutes before adding the peas or beans and spring onions. Put the lid on the pan and let the vegetables sweat, giving them the odd stir, for about ten minutes, with the lid on for half that time. Add the vermouth or wine.

Plop the salmon fillets, skin-down, on top of the vegetables and put the pan, with the lid on, in a pre-heated 200-degree oven for fifteen minutes. Take out, take the lid off, put a splodge of butter on top, grind lots of salt and pepper over everything and spoon out, vegetables at the bottom, salmon on top and some of the delicious cooking juice over that.

Meaty

BUTCHER

FAMILY RUN BUSINESS SINCE 1845

BEANTOWN BEANS
AND BANGERS

Baked beans, fish and chips, and a full English are the tripod of traditional English food. Yet baked beans are no more English than a hot dog. True baked beans come from Beantown, as the rest of America but never the Bostonians, call Boston. How that came to be is a story.

In the way-back-when Boston was a vital part of the Triangle Trade. Sea captains would take on a cargo of sugar cane in Jamaica and sell it in Boston where the cane was refined into sugar, leaving molasses as the waste product. You couldn't sell molasses because people preferred sugar as a sweetener but the canny Bostonians discovered you could distil this sugar waste into rum. The best rum they sold locally and the fiery rotgut they loaded on to the empty ships from Jamaica and sent them off to West Africa where the captains traded the rum with local chiefs in exchange for a cargo of the chief's recently captured neighbours whom they shipped off to Jamaica to spend the rest of their lives cutting sugar cane. That was the Triangle Trade. Or at least it was until William Wilberforce came along.

Bostonians used to supplement their winter diet with beans, a vegetable unknown in Europe before the Columbian Exchange, but which the local Indians used as a carbohydrate source. You could dry the beans, soak them in water and cook them up again months later. The trouble was the rehydrated beans didn't taste that great

until some clever Bostonian thought of putting a few spoons of the cheap and plentiful molasses into his bean stew. And while he was about it, he chucked in some chunks of salt pork, another cheap and plentiful ingredient that kept sweet all through the winter. Bingo. Boston baked beans were born.

Mr Heinz introduced baked beans to England in 1886. They were first sold only in Fortnum's but later became Heinz's most popular English product. Over time the recipe changed. Tomatoes got added to the mixture, sugar got added, molasses was dropped and, then, during the rationing of WW II, the pork disappeared, leaving us with today's Heinz Beanz, a runny, tomato-y confection unrecognisable to a Bostonian. Today you won't find Heinz Baked Beans in a shop in the US unless it specialises in English imports.

When you first try Boston Baked Beans you might get a shock because they are no more like Heinz's than a pork pie is like terrine de sanglier en croute. I love them. Try them and you will too, particularly for a winter weekend lunch dish when a northerly gale is howling outside.

Ingredients for six

+ 500g dried beans, I use haricot
+ 250g smoked pancetta cut into sugar-lump-sized dice
+ 5 tablespoons molasses
+ 3 tablespoons dark brown sugar
+ 3 tablespoons Dijon mustard
+ 2 onions, chopped
+ ½ onion studded with cloves
+ 1 teaspoon ground nutmeg
+ 6 good fat English butcher's sausages or bangers

What you do

Soak the beans in water overnight. Next day drain in a colander. Put the beans in a large casserole, add the pancetta, sugar, mustard, chopped onions, nutmeg and clove-studded onion half. Most people add the molasses now. I do that later because the calcium in the molasses hardens the beans' walls so they take for ever to cook.

Add enough water to come a thumb's thickness over the beans. Put on the stove and bring to the boil uncovered for ten minutes. Top up with water if necessary. Put a lid on the casserole and slip into a 160c oven. The beans will soak up water so take them out to check the water level from time to time. Give them a stir to submerge the crustier beans on top and keep the water just covering the beans.

It's difficult to say how long your beans will take to cook because dried beans can be exceptionally hard if they have been stored for a long time, while fresher ones start out softer. Start testing the beans after three hours or so. If you like them slightly *al dente*, as I do, they should be almost done in four hours; if you like them softer then you may need longer. This is not a dish for the impatient or the deadline-constrained. When they have reached the consistency you like, take them out and add the molasses. Stir the molasses in, add salt and pepper, and give the beans a last half-hour simmering on the stove top with the lid off. Taste for sweetness. Add a bit more molasses if you have a sweet tooth. Don't worry now if the liquid level drops below the bean level. You're aiming for beans in a sticky sauce, not runny English ones.

While the beans have been in the oven you will have cooked your sausages slowly in the oven or on the stove top. Slice each sausage into about six rings. Add these to the beans at the same time as the molasses.

When the beans are just as you like them, put them aside in a cool place and heat them up tomorrow or the next day. They'll taste even better then but if you can't wait that long, go ahead and serve them now. They'll still taste excellent.

This is not a light dish. Serving it with a green salad with a sharp vinaigrette is a good idea and accompanying it with an ice-cold glass of Samuel Adams Boston lager is another.

BOBOTIE

Comfort foods… the ones that put a smile on your face. Yes, you may love sea urchin with ponzu but you don't smile and go aaaah when its is mentioned. Say shepherds' pie, spag bol, or toad in the hole on the other hand and, if you're English, a faraway look of remembered things will light up your face.

Bobotie is one of my favourite comfort foods, one which is hardly known outside South Africa; it's something I can't even pronounce, bobotie. My South African friend, Eduardo, assures me it should be pronounced Baa Boo Tee and who am I to argue with him? It reflects South Africa's unique heritage and combines elements of Dutch, English, and Malay. Next time you are thinking of making a shepherd's pie, do this instead. You won't regret it.

Like so many comfort foods it started as a way of using up leftovers from the weekend roast. You can certainly substitute leftover lamb or beef for fresh in the recipe below. I prefer to use fresh because it has more flavour to impart. Apart from that the non-negotiables for a genuine bobotie are that it must have milk, it must have bread, it must have savoury spices, and dried fruit. Use my recipe as a starting point. You can play around with the details and the proportions to suit yourself…

> "Next time you are thinking of making a shepherd's pie, do this instead. You won't regret it."

Ingredients for four

+ 2 slices stale white bread
+ 250ml whole milk
+ 25g butter
+ 2 onions, chopped
+ 2 garlic cloves, crushed and chopped
+ 700g minced lamb, beef, or pork not too lean (I like half lamb, half pork)
+ 2 tbsp curry powder
+ 6 bay leaves
+ 1 thumb of ginger, chopped small
+ 1 tbsp cardamom pods, crushed
+ 1 tbsp five-spice
+ 2 tbsp spicy mango chutney
+ 1 tbsp Worcester sauce
+ Juice of 1 lemon
+ Pepper and salt
+ 50g sultanas
+ 50g chopped dried apricots
+ 50g toasted flaked almonds
+ 3 eggs

What you do

Put the bread to soak in the milk. Take a big, deep frying pan or, better, a large round shallow le Creuset enamel dish, put it on medium heat and fry the onions until they are soft, adding the garlic halfway through. Take the onions and garlic out and reserve. Turn the heat up a notch, add the meat, crumble it up well with a spatula and stir until it has lost its pinkness. Don't worry if a few bits of meat get charred edges. This whole process of softening the onions and browning the meat should take about fifteen minutes.

Now you add the onions and garlic back in together with whatever spices and flavourings you are using. In my case, curry powder, two of the bay leaves, ginger, cardamom, five-spice, and chutney. You will note that I use tablespoons, not teaspoons, of spice. Bobotie is a dish for the hearty, not the half-hearted. Add the sultanas, apricots, and almonds. Splash in the Worcester sauce, lemon juice, and give everything a good grind of pepper and salt. Mix everything up well. Test for seasoning by taking a spoon of the mixture and frying it in a small pan. Taste and adjust the seasoning and sweetness by adding brown sugar or lemon juice.

Take the bread out of the milk, squeeze it well, tear it into pieces and add to the mixture. Stir. Press the mixture down with a spatula to compress it. This prevents the topping draining into the mixture.

Beat the milk and eggs well. Add pepper and salt. Pour over the meat. Arrange the remaining four bay leaves in a star on the top. Bake in a 180c oven for thirty minutes. Check. The topping should be firm and cooked by now. Switch the oven to grill and finish with five minutes under the grill to brown the top.

Bobotie is good by itself with some peas on the side, like shepherds' pie. People have been known to add tomato ketchup. South Africans usually serve it with rice, yellowed by a spoon of turmeric.

BOILED SHEEP BITS

If I have a favourite recipe it is this. The name exemplifies the Schopenhauer Principle, lower people's expectations in advance and then the actuality will be a wonderful surprise. At 6 pm when your weekend guests say, "Mmm, what's for dinner" and you reply, "Going to be delicious, boiled sheep bits", they run retching from the room and call the local pub to see if they can get a table there instead. But, if they stay, they are generous in their praise.

Why is this so good? Everyone loves lamb and there is nothing better than a garlicky leg of lamb, with crisp golden fat, and roast potatoes. But that does leave you with a heavy stomach and a post-Sunday-lunch feeling afterwards. The wonderful thing about boiled sheep bits is that it is so fresh and clean-tasting.

Nothing is simpler to cook and nothing tastes better.

> "The wonderful thing about boiled sheep bits is that it is so fresh and clean-tasting."

Ingredients for six

+ 2 lamb saddle fillets (Make sure you get this right. The saddle fillet is the eye of a rack of lamb, often called a loin but so is a neck fillet. It is the saddle fillet you want, sometimes known as cannon of lamb, not the neck. You should have a 400g piece of meat about eight inches long and looking like a large salami with no fat on the outside. It may have a bit of membrane. Remove that with a sharp knife.)

What you do

Put the pot you use to cook spaghetti or make stock in on the stove and bring to a gentle boil. The pot should be at least 25 cm high. Put a generous shake of salt in the water. The next bit sounds complicated but you'll find it's easy. Tie some string round one end of each of the lamb fillets. Get a long wooden spoon. Tie the loose end of the string to the wooden spoon so they hang down from it. Slide the fillets into the bubbling water and let them hang there suspended. Your lamb fillets should be just submerged in the water, preferably not touching each other or the bottom. The water should be at a gentle boil.

The fillets will cook in 3 to 4 minutes. After three or so take one out and make an incision to see how cooked it is. Red to very pink is ideal. DO NOT OVERCOOK.

Take both fillets out and leave on a warm, not hot, plate to rest under a cloth while you have your starter. Remember that they will cook a bit more while resting under the cloth.

To serve, slice the lamb into noisettes about 1.5 cm thick. Arrange three of these on each plate and serve with minty new potatoes and a giant splodge of my *Mint Relish (p.170)* together with a simply cooked civilised vegetable like peas or courgettes.

Encourage people to pepper and salt their own lamb. I don't use garlic because the whole idea is to make these fillets the cleanest and purest tasting thing ever. The mint relish brings out the taste, unlike so many dire mint sauces.

CHICKEN SHKMERULI

If you haven't been to Georgia, please go there immediately. Georgia is a small country of fewer than four million people surrounded by bullying and ill-mannered neighbours, Turkey, Azerbaijan, Iran, and, as if that wasn't bad enough, to the North the old grumpy bear itself, Russia. From time to time the bullying neighbours have overrun the country but the Georgians have never let that destroy their national pride and sense of identity. They share our saint, St George, and their flag is a delightful rendition of a St George's cross with four other little crosses on it. The Georgians were civilised Christians well before anyone in West Europe.

The country is beautiful, mountains, rivers, monasteries, mediaeval villages, vineyards, the temperamental Black Sea with the palm-lined city of Batumi on its coast, and then, high in the mountains, Tbilisi, the capital, one of the nicest capitals there is. Despite being squashed by its big neighbours from time to time, the Georgians have kept their independent spirit. They refuse to use Latin script or any of the Cyrillic scripts, let alone Arabic. Instead, they use their Georgian script which no-one else can read and which is all squirly like Tamil in India.

They have wonderful wines, or they say they do, but their quality suffered under fifty years in the Soviet Union and hasn't fully recovered. They have a unique and varied cuisine using fruit, dairy products, walnuts in everything, game, and lots of salads. You eat well in Georgia. I visited it for the second time in 2019 as part of a train trip round the silk route with my honorary goddaughter, Hermione, the brilliant illustrator of this book. We took the mighty Dogu Express sleeper train for twenty-four hours and a thousand miles across Turkey and then headed up into Georgia and Batumi on the Black Sea.

We checked into the charming Hotel Divan in a cobbled street in the Old Town. Obeying the rule of never ask the concierge for a restaurant recommendation because he will send you to a clip joint which gives him a kickback, I asked Timur, the barman, where we should go. Timur, a charming young man who made an excellent cocktail, ignored me as he was busy proposing marriage to 29-year-old Hermione. Hermione said she would think about his proposal and give him her answer in the morning, provided she'd had a very good dinner. "Ah, OK, Meester," said Timur taking his eyes off Hermione for a moment and looking at me for the first time, "in that case, you must take her to the Restaurant Pirosmani and you must eat Chicken Shkmeruli."

We did. How right Timur was. This is one of the simplest but one of the very best chicken dishes. The last time I cooked it, two of the five guests had third helpings, while all had seconds. Luckily, I had cooked enough for eight. It only has three important ingredients, chicken, garlic and milk. You need to eat it to find out how good it is. The next morning when we came to leave, Timur was nowhere to be seen, otherwise Hermione might today be in Batumi, Mrs Timur, cooking Chicken Shkmeruli.

One more thing. Shkmeruli chicken is no stranger to garlic. Possibly not the best thing to have the night before an exciting Tinder date.

"This is one of the simplest but one of the very best chicken dishes. The last time I cooked it, two of the five guests had third helpings, while all had seconds. Luckily, I had cooked enough for eight."

Ingredients for four

+ 6 bone-in, skin-on, chicken thighs (6 because people will want seconds)

+ 2 tbsp vegetable oil

+ 100g butter

+ 12 big garlic cloves, peeled and well squashed in a pestle and mortar, not chopped

+ 300ml whole milk

+ 100ml double cream

+ 100ml crème fraiche

+ 100g walnuts, broken

+ 1 tbsp five-spice powder, or nutmeg (optional, my idea, not pukka but good)

+ Salt and pepper

What you do

Take a large round le Creuset-type casserole (although the Georgians cook this in a flame-proof clay pot), put it on a medium-high heat, and add the oil. Rub good grinds of salt and pepper into the chicken pieces, particularly the skin.

Put the chicken in the casserole, skin side down. You may need to squash the thighs up. Doesn't matter. Regulate the heat so they brown but don't burn. When the skins are crisp and golden, about seven minutes, turn them and brown the other side for a couple of minutes.

Remove the chicken to a plate. Add the butter to the pan which will by now have some chicken fat and scratchings in it. Put the garlic in the pan and stir it well to coat it with the fat. Sauté it for a couple of minutes but don't burn it. Add the milk, double cream and crème fraiche (I like this mixture but you can alter the dairy proportions to suit your taste, just don't use low-fat or single cream as it will split). Bring to a gentle bubble to reduce by a third and to thicken. Don't boil hard or the mixture might curdle. This will take about three minutes. Towards the end throw in the walnut pieces.

Take the pan off the heat and add the chicken thighs, skin side up. Sprinkle the spice on top if you are using it. Spoon some of the milky liquid over the chicken. Put the lid on and bung it in a 200c oven for fifteen to twenty minutes. Take it out when you prick a thigh and the juice runs clear. Spoon a thigh and lots of goo on to each plate. I serve it with my *Lumpy Potatoes (p.147)* and cabbage. I promise you there will be a fight over the last two thighs. You may have to cut them in half.

FINGER-LICKIN' CHICKEN WINGS

Whatever you may think of the Kentucky Colonel's fried chicken (I think it's surprisingly good) the Colonel did hit on one truth. Things taste better eaten in your fingers. Who wants to eat a pizza with knife and fork? Who doesn't like the idea of a picnic? The best part of eating a chicken is picking up a drumstick or wing and chewing away on them till the juice runs down your chin. Burgers? Lamb chops? Scooping up rogan josh in a piece of naan? All finger food. Mmmm…

I came up with this recipe as a homage to the Colonel. My finger-lickin' chicken is healthier than his as it doesn't have a thick coating of batter but I like to think that it's just as more-ish. To be fair, not all of this recipe can be eaten in your fingers unless you fancy scooping up peas and potatoes, but the chicken wings certainly should.

In addition to being finger-friendly, this recipe is one where the vegetables are cooked underneath the chicken so the chicken juices run down and permeate the potatoes and onions making them indescribably delicious.

Ingredients for four

+ 16 chicken wings (don't worry, they'll all be eaten)
+ 5 garlic cloves, chopped small
+ Thumb of ginger, chopped small
+ 1 tbsp Dijon mustard
+ 1 tbsp dried thyme
+ 1 tbsp paprika
+ 3 tbsp olive oil
+ 750g roasting potatoes, peeled and cut into small cubes
+ 2 medium onions, peeled and cut into wedges
+ 400g peas, frozen are fine
+ Salt and pepper

What you do

Mix garlic, ginger, mustard, thyme, paprika, and olive oil, in a big bowl. Throw in the chicken wings and mix them up well with your hands making sure the wings get well-coated in the marinade. If you can leave the wings overnight in the fridge, so much the better but don't worry if you can't.

Boil the potato chunks for two or three minutes in a saucepan, drain, and shake them up well with a lid on the pan to roughen the edges. Put the potatoes and onions in the bottom of a roasting pan, slosh some olive oil over them and toss them, leaving them evenly scattered.

Put the chicken wings on top of the potatoes and onions. You may need two roasting pans for this. It doesn't matter if the wings are touching but they shouldn't be sitting on top of each other. Put the roasting pan(s) in a 200c oven. After twenty minutes take them out, turn the wings over, sprinkle the peas into the pan(s), and replace in the oven. If you are using two pans put the bottom one back on top. Check after another twenty minutes. The wings should be looking charred round the edges but not burnt. You may need another five to ten minutes till they do. Finishing with a few minutes under the grill can be good as long as you don't let things burn.

Give a generous grind of salt and pepper to the dish. Mound potatoes, onions, and peas on each plate. The potatoes should be crisp and slightly burnt. Put the chicken wings in the middle of the table, encouraging people to pick them up in their fingers and start gnawing. A splodge of good chutney for dipping works well.

GERALDINE'S BUGGERED LAMB

Originally this dish was called Delta Dawn Lamb, as it was often cooked on the houseboat of that name on which I live in London. However, I sent the recipe to my friend, Geraldine, who replied shortly afterwards: "Just buggered your lamb. I was distracted by a Zoom call and burnt the lot. And there were a few Jamie Oliver moments, 'If you haven't got it use something else'. And so I used a slug of gin instead of juniper berries and Pineau de Charentes [a sweetish French aperitif wine] instead of Madeira but, phew, I didn't use anything else instead of the lamb. So it was a bit brulé and not as perfect as it could have been but still absolutely delicious. It looked superb on the plate."

That's the kind of cooking I respect. If you don't have one ingredient feel free to substitute. Bravo, Geraldine.

For a winter dinner there is nothing better than Geraldine's Buggered Lamb. Good in spring and autumn too, or whenever the wind is howling outside.

I love lamb. Beef is good, pork is good, but nothing has the flavour of lamb. This is not a universally shared view. Few Americans eat lamb. It has, one hears, "too strong a taste" for the American palate. That's why I love it. I'll take a lamburger over a hamburger any day of the week.

This is one of the simplest and easiest things to cook. You do a little bit of faffing around, pop it in the oven and a few hours later you have a dinner that has people mopping their plates. It's also dead cheap.

Ingredients for four

+ 2kg lamb shoulder on the bone

+ 2 large onions peeled and cut into quarters

+ 4 big banana shallots, halved lengthwise but not peeled

+ 3 carrots diced

+ 2 sticks celery chopped

+ 8 garlic cloves, tailed, but kept whole and not skinned

+ 15 juniper berries crushed

+ Salt and pepper

+ 500ml medium sweet Madeira (Duke of Clarence is good)

For marinade

+ 6 salted anchovy fillets, chopped

+ 100ml ketjaap manis (Indonesian sweet soy-based sauce – if unavailable use soy sauce and 2 tablespoons of brown sugar, but won't be as good)

+ 1 tbsp dried thyme

+ 1 tbsp dried oregano

+ 2 tsp ground cloves

+ 2 tsp Chinese five spice powder

+ Juice of 1 lemon

+ 100ml dry white vermouth or fino sherry (dry white wine as a back-up)

+ 1 tbsp black treacle (molasses)

What you do

Marinade part:

I'm sceptical as to whether overnight marinating really makes a difference. With this lamb it's worth it, but if you don't have time and can only put the marinade on even as little as half an hour in advance it will still be good.

Remove any obvious lumps of hard fat from the lamb but leave plenty of surface fat. It's where the flavour comes from. Score the lamb on both sides with a sharp knife cutting at least 1 cm into the flesh. Score it both ways so you end up with scored diamonds about 3 cm by 3 cm.

Put all the marinade ingredients in a bowl and mix them up well with a spoon. Taste the marinade and adjust for sweetness with brown sugar or lemon juice.

Put the lamb, underside up, in the roasting tin you will cook it in. Spoon a tablespoon of marinade over it, rubbing it in with the back of the spoon. Repeat all over the underside until you've used almost half the marinade. Flip the lamb and repeat the process with the skin side using your spoon to work the rest of the marinade into the diamond scoring. Use all the marinade. Some of the marinade will run off into the roasting pan. Don't worry about it. Leave the lamb in a cool place or the fridge for at least half-an-hour, longer if you have the time.

Cooking part

Heat oven to 220c.

Take the marinaded lamb out of the roasting pan, leaving any excess marinade in the bottom. Spread the other ingredients across the bottom of the pan, making sure the shallots are cut side up. You won't need oil as the lamb fat will soon melt and drip down. Put the lamb on top of the vegetables, skin side up. Give it a good grind of pepper and a sprinkle of sea salt (it doesn't need much salt because of the anchovies and soy).

Put the lamb in the middle of the oven. You are starting at a high heat to brown the top of the meat. After 20 minutes turn the heat down to 160c, remove the lamb, cover it loosely with foil, and move it to the bottom of the oven. After two hours, take the foil off, add the Madeira, spoon some of the melted marinade over the top, and return it to the bottom of the oven to cook uncovered.

The lamb will need at least three hours at 160c. I try to cook mine for five hours by which time the meat has retreated from the ends of the bone and can be shredded with a spoon.

Take the roasting pan out, pour off the gravy into a separate pot and put this somewhere to cool, even in the fridge if you're in a hurry, while leaving the lamb and vegetables under some foil or a tea towel in a warming drawer. When the gravy is cold it will have a thick layer of solidified white lamb fat on top. Use a spoon to remove the fat and discard it. Warm the gravy up again in a saucepan and taste. It should be a delicious mix of marinade, Madeira, and lamb drippings. Add whatever you think it needs to make the sweetness and saltiness right for you.

Put the lamb on a carving board and hack it up into chunks and strips. You may find a fork a better tool for this than a knife. Discard any big blobs of fat but leave the crisp bits. Get a big oval or round warmed serving bowl and heap the lamb in the middle. Arrange the vegetables around the edge. Pour a quarter of the gravy over the top and keep the rest in a pouring pot to go on the table for people to help themselves.

I usually serve this with my *Lumpy Potatoes (p. 147)* and *Cabbage Is King (p.142)*.

POULET AU MUSCAT

What is it about cooking a chicken in wine that makes people demand it be *un coq*, not *une poule*. It is probably that monsieur le coq is a muscular old bully who needs long cooking to make him edible while his *poule de luxe* ex-girlfriends surrender their charms more easily. One of my favourite recipes is **Red-Eye Coq (p.126)**. It is plate-moppingly good but it is a cold weather recipe. It's not something you would want to eat on a hot August day. Coq au Muscat on the other hand is a perfect summer dish. Eat it sitting on the terrace under your favourite olive tree on a warm summer evening.

You will find lots of recipes for Coq au Riesling, the best-known being Nigel Slater's, and very good it is too. Mine is similar but has a few differences. I use muscat wine which has the wonderful rich floral scent of over-ripe grapes. Most muscats are very sweet, too sweet for this dish. I use a dry muscat I get from the Wine Society. It is perfect for this. If you can't find a dry muscat then by all means use an Alsatian pinot gris or, failing that, Riesling. The other main difference is that I use half chicken stock and half wine for the liquid, not all wine. This gives the sauce a wonderful depth of flavour.

Ingredients for four

+ 8 boneless chicken thighs
+ 1 large or 2 small onions, sliced
+ 200g pancetta sliced into sticks
+ 4 garlic cloves, sliced
+ 8 button mushrooms, halved
+ 200g peas, frozen is fine
+ 300ml chicken stock (not a cube)
+ 300ml dry muscat or similar wine, preferably from Alsace
+ Butter, olive oil
+ Salt and pepper

What you do

Take a large round lidded casserole dish, the 30cm Le Creuset one is ideal, and put it on a medium heat. Add a good splodge of olive oil and another of butter. Add the onions, garlic, and pancetta and fry gently until the onion softens and the bacon has rendered up much of its fat, probably ten minutes. Don't brown the onions or garlic. When ready, take everything out and keep warm.

Add a little more oil and butter if necessary and brown the chicken pieces over medium-high heat, around four minutes on the skin side and two on the other side. The skin should be golden, not dark.

Spoon out excess fat as you want the dish to be fresh-tasting, not oily. Add the reserved onion mixture back to the pan and pour over the stock and wine. Give everything a good stir, turn the heat down to medium, and add the mushrooms and peas. Season with salt and pepper. Put the lid on the pan and leave to simmer over medium or medium-low heat. Check after two minutes that it is not boiling which will toughen the chicken and make the wine bitter. It should be at a gentle bubble, not a rolling boil.

If you have a tender poulet, which I recommend, the dish will be ready in about fifteen minutes. If it's a muscular old coq he might need twice that. Take a piece out, cut a bit off and check. If you cut through the meat should be white, not pink. When everything is ready take the pieces out and halve them before returning to the pan. This makes them more wieldy on the plate. I don't halve the pieces earlier because small pieces tend to toughen up more than big ones. Feel free to sprinkle some chopped parsley over the top. You could add a splosh of cream. I don't because the dish is rich enough already.

This is best served in soup plates with crusty bread for mopping and a spoon as well as a knife and fork for scooping up juices.

ROADKILL CHICKEN

Sorry about the name of this recipe but your chicken will look as if it's been run over. It will however taste delicious. There are many ways of roasting a chicken, nearly all of them good but a perennial problem is how do you cook a chicken so that the thighs are fully cooked without the breast drying out. Roadkill chicken is a good answer.

You butterfly or spatchcock your chicken. While you do not want to butterfly everything, I am a fan of doing it on a selective basis. A leg of lamb is delicious but it's always tricky keeping it pink in the middle without it going grey on the outside. The advantage of butterflying something, taking out the bones and spreading the deboned chicken, turkey, or lamb leg, out flat, is that it cooks more evenly. So it is with Roadkill Chicken although in this case you only remove the backbone. Both the legs and the breast will be cooked just right.

Roadkill Chicken has another advantage. The vegetables you put under the chicken will be permeated with the delicious chicken juices that run down as it cooks.

Ingredients for four

+ 1 medium chicken

+ 2 onions, peeled and chopped into wedges

+ 500g waxy potatoes, diced into small cubes

+ 250g peas, frozen are fine

+ 2 medium carrots, diced

+ 200g lardons

+ 4 garlic cloves, peeled and halved

+ 2 tsp dried thyme

+ 1 tbsp olive oil

+ 200ml Madeira

+ Salt and pepper

What you do

Put the chicken breast down on a chopping board. Using poultry shears or a sharp knife, cut out the backbone by cutting about 2 cm either side of the middle. Discard the backbone, turn the chicken over and with the heel of your hand push down on the breastbone to flatten the chicken. You will hear some clicks as you push hard. The squashed-down chicken will look like a giant frog.

Scatter the vegetables and lardons evenly over the bottom of a roasting pan. Sprinkle the olive oil over them. Put the flattened chicken on top of the vegetables, breast-side up. Spread a generous amount of sea salt over the chicken, patting it in with your hand. The salt will ensure a crisp skin. Sprinkle the thyme over everything and give it a grind of pepper.

Slide the roasting pan into the middle of a 220c oven. After twenty minutes, take out the pan and add the Madeira. Replace in middle of the oven. Take it out after 45 minutes. The skin should be a deep golden-brown. Test by putting a fork into the thickest part of the thigh to see if the juices run clear. If they are still pink, put the chicken back for another ten minutes or so.

When done, take the pan out and put the chicken on a carving-board under some foil for a ten-minute rest. Scoop out everything else with a slotted spoon and place round the edges of a warmed oval platter. Pour the gravy from the chicken juice and Madeira into a jug and keep warm while you carve the chicken. To carve, remove the legs and then detach the drumsticks from the thighs. Remove the wings, leaving a nugget of breast meat attached. I prefer to serve the breasts in chunks rather than slices. To do this, run your knife along the breastbone on one side and then cut under the breast and slide the knife further down allowing you to remove the breast in one piece. Repeat on the other side. Cut both breasts into chunks by cutting across the breast at one-inch intervals.

Take the platter and pile the chicken pieces in the middle surrounded by vegetables. Serve with a green vegetable. Pour a good splodge of gravy over each serving.

NO BUN
BURGER

Just as every Englishman thinks he can make perfect scrambled eggs, every American has the one and only best burger recipe. Its name came of course from Hamburg. Hamburgers (the people, not the beef patty) have excellent local beef and for centuries they have been chopping it up, mixing it with good things like onions and garlic, popping it on the grill, and serving it up as a Hamburg Steak. Hamburg was the port of embarkation for the great wave of German emigrants to the U.S. All would have seen Hamburg Steak on the menu of the ships that took them to America and it was not long before posh New York and Philadelphia restaurants were also serving Hamburg Steak, pretty much a cooked steak tartare.

Americans love to eat on the go, hence their desire to make everything portable by clapping a couple of bits of bread round it and turning it into a sandwich. This proclivity to ensandwich everything but dessert may also account for American obesity. There is a debate as to who turned the Hamburg Steak into the Hamburger by popping it between the two cheeks of a bun but it was White Castle, the first US fast food chain in the 1920s, that popularised it.

Because I share the Americans' propensity for obesity, I try not to have the bun and go for a German style Hamburg steak instead of the American hamburger sandwich. It's a matter of personal taste but I also think it is a pity to add cheese, bacon, tomato, lettuce, ketchup, mustard, and a pickled gherkin to a simple grilled burger. Too many textures, too many tastes. Keep it simple and go for quality. Here's my recipe for a burger but, please, it's just my recipe for a juicy, flavourful piece of grilled chopped meat, I'm not trying to claim it's the genuine article.

Ingredients for four burgers

+ 750g minced beef. Don't go for "lean", you need fat for flavour; lean is 5% fat; go for 10% to 15% fat and don't get meat that's been too finely minced; it should look more like the chopped beef for steak tartare

+ Vegetable oil

+ 1 big onion, finely chopped

+ 3 spring onions, finely chopped, white bits only

+ Small handful of pine nuts

+ 1 tsp cumin*

+ 1 tsp ground ginger*

+ 1 tsp five spice*

+ 1 tsp dried thyme or fresh equivalent

+ 1 large egg

+ 2 tbsp Guinness or Madeira

+ Several dashes of Worcester sauce

+ Good grinds of salt and pepper

*These are spices I like for zing and flavour; feel free to leave them out or substitute others

What you do

Sauté the onion (not the spring onions) until soft but not brown, about five minutes. Put the beef in a bowl and add all the other ingredients including the onion. Mix it around with your hands. Take it out and form it into four patties the thickness of a 300-page hardback.

Heat a thick non-stick pan over medium high heat and add a small splodge of oil. I don't do mine on a barbecue as mine lack the breadcrumbs that bind together conventional burgers, making them more prone to falling apart if not treated gently, although the egg does act as a binding agent. Gently slip your four burgers into the pan. After three minutes flip them and give them another two minutes on the other side. The outside should be crusty and the inside juicy and rare.

You could put these into a bun and add tomato and lettuce and whatever but I eat mine with a knife and fork on a plate. Ketchup on the side is good. So is anything yoghurty like raita or tzatziki. I'd forget the lettuce and tomato and eat your burger with grilled vegetables.

KNOB CREEK PHEASANT

Pheasants today taste like chickens did before battery farming was developed. Full of flavour but not gamey. No-one today hangs them for days, unless they have shot them themselves, because most people buy them from the butcher, plucked and dressed. You can only hang a game bird while it's still got its feathers on. I love pheasant. It's my convenience food. Costs less than a hamburger, bung it in the oven, take it out 45 minutes later and tuck in. Less effort than Marks & Spencer's ready-to-cook Mexican fajitas.

People think pheasant is going to be dry because that's what the cookbooks tell you. That's because one generation of cooking writers copies out the previous generation's recipes. Pheasants used to be lean when they were wild birds. Today a pheasant you buy at your butcher will be a reared bird that has been released into "the wild" in June but which knows where to go every evening to get a cropful of corn which the keeper has provided. The result is that the modern pheasant is fatter and juicier than its genuinely born-in-the-wild predecessor. Cookery-writers' obsession with basting and putting strips of bacon on top to "stop it drying out" are unnecessary unless you overcook your bird in which case, give it to the dog.

There are lots of ways of cooking pheasant, none of them bad. Most good chicken recipes work well for pheasant.

Here's one of my favourites, the drunken raisins making it that little bit different.

"...the modern pheasant is fatter and juicier than its genuinely born-in-the-wild predecessor. Cookery-writers' obsession with basting and putting strips of bacon on top to "stop it drying out" are unnecessary unless you overcook your bird in which case, give it to the dog."

Ingredients for four

+ 2 large pheasants

+ 2 handfuls of raisins

+ 200ml of Knob Creek bourbon – or any other good bourbon; if you want to substitute rum, calvados, or Scotch go ahead but it won't be as good

+ Sprinkle of fennel seed

+ 200ml chicken stock

What you do

Heat your oven to 200c. Soak the raisins in a bowl with the bourbon for ten to fifteen minutes. Put the pheasants in a roasting tin, up-end them, and stuff them with the raisins, followed by pouring the remaining bourbon into them from the bowl. Some of the bourbon will leak out when you put the pheasants down. Good. Put the pheasants in the roasting pan breast upward. Give the breasts and the legs a very good grind of salt and pat that into the skin. This will help you get crisp skin. I usually sprinkle some fennel seeds over the bird. Roast pheasants, and chickens, seem to have an affinity with fennel seed.

Pop pheasants in the oven. After the birds have been in the oven for 20 minutes, take them out and add the stock to the pan. I usually upend the pheasant using an oven glove and pour the stock through the birds so it picks up their flavour. Put them back in the oven.

They will take 45 minutes to an hour to cook depending on how big they are. After 45 minutes take them out and make a cut between the leg and the body to see how cooked the birds are. If they're still pink put them back in. Pheasant, like chicken, should not be served pink.

When they are cooked, take them out, put a cloth on top of them and leave them to rest while you eat your starter.

Carving tip. Cut off the entire leg and then separate drumstick from thigh. I tend not to eat the drumsticks as they are full of tough tendons and I'm too lazy to pull them out although they are good for gnawing when cold. I don't cut the breast into slices in the normal way. Instead I slide the knife along the breastbone and remove each breast in one piece. Then cut it sideways across the breast into three or four pieces. That way each piece should have some crisp skin on top of it and cutting across the grain makes it taste better.

Taste the gravy. By now the bourbon should have picked up some pheasant taste. Spoon some over the birds for serving.

I usually serve this with *Cabbage Is King (p.142)* and some quartered Cox's apples which I sauté with their skins on with a bit of honey and ground ginger until they are just softening. *Lumpy Potatoes (p.147)* go well with pheasant.

Redcurrant jelly or cranberry sauce on the side is fine but if you go into your local deli you may find some bottled Polish bilberries. These too make a good accompaniment.

LAZY MAN'S COQ

Red-Eye Coq (p. 126) recipe has given its name to this book. It's easy to make but it does involve a bit of faffing around. If you are not in a mood to faff or only want to feed two people, Lazy Man's Coq takes a minimum of effort and tastes terrific. It also gives you some crispy skin.

Ingredients for two

+ 4 boneless skin-on chicken thighs
+ Oil and butter
+ 125g lardons
+ 3 garlic cloves, bashed and sliced
+ 12 tiny onions, peeled, otherwise two medium onions, peeled and cut into wedges
+ 150g button mushrooms, halved unless tiny
+ 1 tsp thyme dried or 2 tsp fresh
+ Salt and pepper
+ 150ml chicken stock
+ 150ml hearty red wine
+ 1tbsp molasses

What you do

Take a heavy-bottomed round casserole and add a good glug of oil and a splodge of butter over medium-high heat. Put the thighs skin down in the pan to brown well. That will take five minutes or a bit more. Flip the thighs so they are skin side up. Throw in the lardons, garlic, and onions. Add the stock, wine, and molasses. Pop the casserole into a 200c oven. Take out after fifteen minutes and add the mushrooms, thyme and season. Return to oven.

Take out after another fifteen minutes and test the chicken for doneness. There shouldn't be any pink meat. Taste for seasoning and balance.

Take the chicken thighs out and cut into bite size pieces. Return them to the pan and ladle out into soup plates. Eat with a spoon and some crusty bread.

LOOKS ODD, TASTES SUBLIME, ROAST CHICKEN

One of the many wonderful things the Bolognese do is to cook pork loin in milk. The milk curdles and by the time you come to serve it the sauce has broken down into grey curds. Doesn't look great but, wow, does it taste good. I cooked this a couple of times and if you want to try it look no further than Marcella Hazan's classic recipe. Then I thought, "Well, if it works for pork, why not for chicken", and discovered that Jamie Oliver had got there before me. In his usual understated style, he calls his the "best roast chicken ever". Hard to disagree. My recipe is inspired by his with a few modifications. Jamie, old cock, feel free to steal one of my recipes any time you want.

Ingredients for four burgers

+ 1 large free-range butcher's chicken, untrussed
+ Olive oil
+ 1 lemon
+ 100g lardons
+ 10 cloves of garlic (topped and tailed but not peeled)
+ Nutmeg
+ 500ml of full-cream milk (I use half full cream milk and half single cream)

What you do

Heat the oven to 190c. Put a thick round or oval Le Creuset casserole dish on the hob over medium-high heat and add a good shot of olive oil. Take the zest off the lemon with a peeler and chop the peel into small bits. Rub salt on to the chicken. Put the chicken into the casserole and brown it well on all sides. This will take about ten minutes. Take the chicken out and pour off the fat while trying to hold on to the brown bits. Chop the peeled lemon into quarters and stuff the chicken with them.

Add the milk, cream, lemon zest, garlic cloves and lardons to the pot. Put the chicken back into the pot, breast up. Grate a good amount of nutmeg on to the chicken and into the sauce. Grind some pepper over the chicken. Cut out a large square of baking parchment paper and pop this on to cover the chicken, tucking it down the sides a bit (not essential but it will help keep it juicy).

Put chicken in the oven, lid off. Lower the heat to 180 after an hour. Baste the chicken with the sauce a couple of times if you remember. Take it out after 1 ½ hours. Check by pulling a thigh clear from the body that it is fully cooked. There should be no pink anywhere. The sauce will be chiefly greyish curds. Don't worry about how it looks. It will taste awesome.

Take the chicken out and carve it into joints and chunks. I serve it with *Lumpy Potatoes (p. 147)* and *Cabbage Is King (p.142)*. Spoon lots of sauce over the chicken and serve, giving everyone a couple of garlic cloves to squash with their forks. The insides will come out like toothpaste, soft and sweet.

111

LOMBARD LAMB STEW

Lombardy is the richest region of Italy, occupying as it does a large chunk of the northwest with rich Milan plop in the middle of it. Its cuisine has more in common with its neighbours France and Switzerland than it does with the olive oil and tomato-heavy cooking of southern Italy. Lombards use butter and cream more than olive oil. Olives don't grow in most of Lombardy.

They have a rich cuisine, with gooey cheeses like gorgonzola and creamy risottos redolent with truffle.

It may seem odd therefore that this simplest and plainest of all recipes comes from Lombardy. It's not as odd as its sounds because the Lombards have something else in common with their transalpine neighbours. They are hard-working.

While the Romans sit in cafes arguing about politics all day, the Neapolitans spend their time murdering cousins, and the Tuscans admiring the view, the Lombards are hard at work in factories and offices. As a result, a feature of not having much time to cook, Lombards often make simple, one-pot dishes which require little work.

Nothing is simpler and requires less hands-on cooking than Lombard Lamb Stew. It is also cheap. It is made from shoulder, it has minimal additions to it, just a small handful of everyday vegetables, and no flavouring to speak of apart from a juniper berry or two. Few things look more appealing than the ingredients of this stew in the casserole dish before you put it on the stove; few things look less appetising than the stew four hours later, fully cooked. Unlike in most stew recipes, you don't brown the meat first, you don't soften the vegetables in a sauté pan, and you add nothing to enrich the sauce. The surprise is that nothing is richer and more rewarding than the end product. If you like the taste of lamb, you will go crazy over this. If you don't like lamb or consider its taste too strong, better pop out for a Big Mac.

This recipe involves virtually no work. Marcella Hazan, the woman who did for Italian cooking in America what Julia Childs did for French, has a good recipe for this. Mine is mainly pirated from her with a few tweaks.

Ingredients for four

+ Lamb shoulder (this has too many bones for you to chop up at home unless you are an axe-murderer so get your butcher to saw it up into 3-inch chunks, most of them on-the-bone; you need the bones for flavour)

+ 2 medium carrots diced

+ 1 medium onion chopped

+ 1 celery stick chopped

+ 250ml white wine or dry vermouth

+ 3 cloves garlic skinned and squashed

+ 3 sprigs rosemary (or 1 tbsp dried rosemary)

+ 1 tbsp crushed juniper berries

+ Salt and pepper

What you do

Nothing could be simpler than cooking this as there is literally nothing to do apart from popping it into a suitable pot. Put all the ingredients into a cast-iron or enamel casserole and put it on a medium-low heat with the lid on with a good grind of salt and pepper. From time to time, take the lid off and turn the pieces over so the bottom pieces come to the top and vice versa. For most of the cooking process the lamb, not having been browned, will look an unappetising grey colour. Don't worry. It won't when you've finished.

After two hours, turn the heat to medium and shift the lid slightly to one side. The lamb will have given off a lot of liquid by now. Give it at least another 1½ hours, preferably two at the higher heat. The liquid should be bubbling gently but not boiling furiously. Finally, after a total of 3½ to 4 hours total cooking time your Lombard Lamb Stew should be ready. Most of the liquid should have evaporated by now. The lamb, which will have gone a rich brown and more or less disintegrated, should be coated in a thick sauce. If there is still a lot of liquid, take the top off, remove the lamb as you don't want it to disintegrate, and turn the heat up to reduce the sauce.

You can now serve it up, maybe with some sauté potatoes and cabbage. First, I take the lamb pieces out and put them on a chopping board so I can remove the blobby bits of fat while leaving the soft, melting bits. Most of the fat will have melted into the thick sauce by then. That done, pop the lamb pieces back into the pot, stir well to coat with sauce and serve it up on warm plates. Your guests will be astonished at the concentrated richness of the taste. Find a wine with hair on its chest to go with it, maybe from Sicily or Calabria.

NO CHOUCROUTE
CHOUCROUTE

Everyone knows, and some people love, choucroute, the dish that defines Alsatian cooking. Every restaurant in every village in the rolling vineyard hills between Strasbourg and Colmar serves its own home-made choucroute. Choucroute of course is the fermented cabbage itself, known as sauerkraut across the Rhine in Germany. You can serve choucroute with just about anything from fish to fowl but *le vrai choucroute* is Alsace's choucroute garnie, choucroute served with the wonderful products of Mr Pig, Alsatian sausages, chunks of ham, and pork belly. Of all France's great regional dishes, choucroute may be the one that has spread least in the Anglo-Saxon world. That may be because the Anglo-Saxon world is ambivalent about sauerkraut, shredded cabbage long-fermented in salt, first cousin to Korea's kimchi. I love it but many people don't.

That disappoints me because there are few more convivial dishes for a chilly evening's supper

than choucroute, layered with wonderful pork bits. I seldom serve it though, because too many people don't like the sauerkraut.

And then I came up with a cunning plan. Sauerkraut is fermented cabbage. Why not use fresh cabbage instead? Everyone likes fresh cabbage if it is nicely cooked. Hence this recipe.

A word about the things you put with your cabbage. Sausages are essential. English pork sausages don't work in this; they would be as out of place as a Yorkshireman in Naples. Find wonderful French and German sausages, probably not Italian, although Polish would be OK. There's nothing wrong with starting with the humble frankfurter, as long as you get good German ones, not something made as hot dog pap. It's up to you what you use in addition to sausages. For me pork belly is essential but you can also add leaner cuts of pork and ham. Black pudding is another possibility. Your call.

Ingredients for four

+ 2 cabbages, Savoy is best, cored and shredded

+ 2 crisp apples, Cox is good, cored and sliced, skin on

+ 150ml off-dry Alsace wine (pinot gris or gewürztraminer)

+ 2 onions, peeled and cut into chunks

+ 12 new potatoes, quartered

+ 4 cloves garlic, squashed and chopped

+ 2 tbsp caraway seeds

+ 2 tbsp juniper berries, squashed

+ 2 tbsp goose fat or olive oil

+ 8 sausages, mixed selection such as frankfurter, bratwurst, boudin blanc or noir, weisswurst

+ 4 extra thick slices of pork belly, sliced into two-inch chunks

+ Optional chunks or thick slices of ham or pork

What you do

I cook the cabbage and apple separately to the other ingredients and mix them up at the end.

Heat the oven to 200c. Spread the potatoes, onion and garlic in a lightly oiled roasting pan. Scatter the sausages, pork belly and whatever other pork products you are using on top. Give everything a grind of salt and pepper. Put the pan in the middle of the oven. The juices from the melting fat in the pork belly will run down and be soaked up by the potatoes and onions which will taste wonderful as a result. Take out after fifteen minutes and turn the pork pieces over. Replace in the oven for another ten minutes. Take out and test that the potatoes and onions are fully cooked. If not, remove and reserve the meat and give the potatoes and onions another ten minutes in the oven. (If you want to, you can put the potatoes in boiling water for three minutes before putting them in the oven to make sure they are cooked.) When done, leave the pan to keep warm.

Now for the cabbage. Heat your biggest frying pan or wok to medium. Add the goose fat or oil. Throw in the apple slices and cook while stirring for five minutes, then turn the heat up to high and add the shredded cabbage. It will threaten to overflow the pan but don't worry, it will soon reduce in size. Pour the Alsace wine over the cabbage. Stir-fry the cabbage and apple slices while adding the caraway seeds and juniper berries together with a grind of pepper and a big grind of salt. Continue to toss the cabbage over high heat while the wine cooks off. Taste some shreds of cabbage after five minutes. When they are al dente, neither crisp nor soggy, turn the heat down to very low and add the potatoes, onion, and pork from the roasting tin along with the melted fat from the pork belly.

Mix everything up well and transfer to a serving platter. Arrange it so you have sausages sticking out at inviting angles. Put the platter in the middle of the table and invite people to help themselves. Make sure there is Dijon mustard to go with the sausages. Serve with an Alsatian white wine, probably *pinot gris*, *pinot blanc*, or a dry muscat, rather than Riesling or Gewürztraminer.

NOT SHEPHERD'S PIE

Who doesn't like shepherd's pie? It's the ultimate comfort food, the quintessential English dish, and the housewife's answer to what to do with the leftovers from the roast. You can make it with beef or lamb, raw or cooked, the vegetables, carrots, celery, and onions are standard, with a slight debate as to whether to add tomatoes (I don't), and a dash or two of Worcester Sauce. Put a wodge of mashed potato on top of that, bung it in the oven for a bit and bingo, you have your shepherd's pie.

My mum used to make a great shepherd's pie. So did yours.

But yet… but yet… shepherd's pie is lovely and comforting but, let's face it, it doesn't get too far off the runway as far as being a great dish is concerned. It can be a bit ordinary.

Umami may be a word that annoys many of you, in which case skip this paragraph, but umami lies at the heart of so many of the best things to eat. If you have to translate it people usually use the word "savoury" but it's more than that. Shepherd's pie is good but it can be lacking in umami; ragu alla Bolognese on the other hand is loaded with it.

My "Not Shepherd's Pie" would give a traditionalist a conniption. No English shepherd would recognise it. I have borrowed elements such as milk from Bologna, so strictly speaking it's Bolognese Shepherd's Pie. And it has umami. I've also borrowed the "secret ingredients", instant coffee and molasses, from the **Red-Eye Coq (p.126)** recipe to add depth and richness to the sauce. Sometimes I add a splodge of wonderful Indonesian ketjap manis for extra depth and umami but you don't have to so I've left it out of the recipe. It may make it too sweet for some people.

You can do two things with Not Shepherd's Pie. You can put mashed potato on the top and bung it in a hot oven for a tip-top Pie. Or you can cook some spaghetti or tagliatelle and use it as the sauce. This is such a rich dish and so full of umami that I think pasta is the way to go. Your choice.

> **"Umami may be a word that annoys many of you, in which case skip this paragraph, but umami lies at the heart of so many of the best things to eat."**

Ingredients for four

+ 500g minced or chopped lamb (shoulder is good because of the lean-fat mix); ready-minced is OK but chopping the meat into a fine dice will give you a better texture. (The Bolognese often use pork, Bologna being a pork-loving town; if you want to do 300g lamb and 200g pork sausage meat, go ahead)

+ Splodge of olive oil and of butter

+ 4 carrots, diced

+ 2 medium onions, chopped

+ 2 sticks of celery, finely diced

+ 3 cloves of garlic, finely chopped

+ 200ml white wine (red is OK but not what the Bolognese use)

+ 200ml milk

+ 125ml strong stock (lamb, beef or chicken)

+ 2 tsp fresh thyme, if using dried halve the quantity

+ 2 tsp fresh rosemary, chopped, if using dried halve the quantity

+ 1 tsp instant coffee

+ 1 tbsp molasses

+ Big splodge of Worcester sauce

+ Bigger splodge of tomato ketchup

What you do

Heat a large frying pan or wok to medium and throw in the lamb with a splodge of oil and of butter. Break the meat up and stir it. Let a crust form and then break up again. Repeat. After five minutes it will be brown and the melted lamb fat and cooking fats will have formed a pool of liquid. Remove from heat and pour off most of the liquid fat (thereby getting rid of a big chunk of calories).

Return the pan to the heat and add the carrots, onion, celery and garlic to the meat. Leave these to soften with the occasional stir. After five minutes add the wine, stock and milk. Turn the heat up and let it bubble away till the liquid has reduced by half or more and is starting to look syrupy. This may take ten minutes. Add the thyme, rosemary, Worcester sauce, ketchup, coffee, and molasses. Add a good grind of pepper and salt.

Cook this for five minutes on a high heat and then lower to just above a simmer. In theory this will be "ready" after an hour or so bubbling away at a simmer but if you give yourself plenty of time by starting early so you can simmer it for two or three hours, it will taste even better. You don't need to do anything while it is simmering apart from the odd stir. I usually cover the pan for half of the period as I don't want to lose too much liquid.

Taste from time to time and adjust seasoning. I like the natural sweetness the milk, vegetables, and molasses give it but if that is too sweet for you, you could squeeze in some lemon juice. If it gets too dry, add a little stock if you have some left, otherwise, water.

Now, if it's Shepherd's Pie you're after, remove the mixture and pour it into an oven dish and smooth it out. Then take the mashed potato you made while the mixture was simmering and spread that over the top. Please, not too much. Shepherd's Pie does not need an inch and a half of spud smothering it, half an inch is fine.

Put this in the top of a 200c oven for twenty minutes or until the top starts to brown, take out, and serve on warm plates.

OR, Make enough spaghetti or tagliatelle for four and use the mixture as sauce for the pasta. Grate lots of parmesan, pure umami, over it. That's my favourite way.

OXTAIL STEW FOR A COLD JANUARY DAY

When I was little my mother used to make oxtail stew and I loved it. I can't remember if she made it because during rationing it was easier to get hold of oxtail than steak, or whether it was because oxtail was cheap, but I don't remember her making it when I became a teenager. More's the pity.

My other contact with oxtail is through Heinz. It is ironic that Heinz, that most American of companies, has given us three British classics which we all love, Heinz Baked Beans, Oxtail Soup and Cream of Tomato Soup. These are things that bring a smile to the face of any Brit. I suspect that if you want to buy them in America, you will only find them in British specialty shops.

Here's my version of oxtail stew. Many people add tomatoes, or tomato paste. I love tomatoes but surely not in a dish as Anglo-Saxon as this? The question of what liquid to use is a subject of debate: stock or wine or indeed water? I compromise by using equal quantities of stock, wine, and stout.

You can take the stewing vegetables out an hour before the end and replace them with fresh vegetables which will be firmer. I don't because I like the melting texture of the carrot and the turnip which have gone the full three hours, but go ahead if you want freshness and crunch.

Potatoes. You can put spuds chopped up in the stew but they don't really work. Serving this with mashed potatoes is a better idea.

> "The question of what liquid to use is a subject of debate: stock or wine or indeed water? I compromise by using equal quantities of stock, wine, and stout."

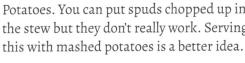

Ingredients for four

+ Big glug of oil, one which can stand high heat
+ ½ cup plain flour
+ 1 oxtail which your butcher will have chopped into six or seven pieces
+ 3 carrots, roughly chopped
+ 2 celery sticks, roughly chopped
+ 1 onion, peeled and quartered
+ I turnip, chopped
+ 10 cloves of garlic, unpeeled.
+ 500ml beef stock (chicken or water if you don't have beef)
+ 500ml Guinness or, better if you can get it, Sam Smith's Imperial Stout
+ 500ml red wine
+ Big dash of Worcester sauce
+ 10 to 15 tiny white onions peeled, if unavailable, two onions, peeled and cut into wedges
+ 10 button mushrooms, halved
+ 1 tsp dried thyme
+ 10 to 15 juniper berries, crushed
+ Salt and pepper

What you do

Cut as much fat as you can off the oxtail pieces. Put the flour in a bag, add the oxtail pieces and shake them around to coat them. Heat the oil to medium-high in a big frying pan or wok, throw in the oxtail pieces having shaken off any excess flour. Brown them all over. It'll take five to ten minutes.

Take the oxtail out and reserve while you throw the chopped onion, celery, turnip, and carrot into the hot oil from the oxtail. Stir them around for five minutes or so till they pick up some colour.

Decant the vegetables into a big round Le Creuset cast-iron enamel casserole or similar, add the oxtail pieces, the garlic cloves, and the liquids. Bring to a boil briefly, then turn down to a low simmer. Let it simmer away, bubbling gently for three hours or so.

Take out the oxtail pieces, let them cool enough so that you can handle them, and strip off as much meat as you can while discarding the fat and gelatine. You'll be surprised how little meat there is but don't worry. The meat is not the point. The soup is the point and all the flavour from the bones, meat and gelatine has gone into that.

Put the meat back in the stew and add the small onions (peeling them is easy if you blanch them briefly in boiling water and then cool them under cold water), the mushrooms, and thyme. Stir, taste, and season with salt and pepper.

Simmer for another half-hour, taste, adjust seasoning and serve. Goes well with *Cabbage Is King (p.142)*. My mother used to make delicious suet dumplings to go in this. I would too but I'm lazy so maybe you should go with *Lumpy Potatoes (p.147)*.

PADDY O'MILO'S IRISH STEW

This is another example of peasant cooking at its best; the more people try to tart up peasant dishes the less interesting they become, whether they be cassoulet, coq au vin, or paella. Peasant dishes are made with whatever cheap ingredients are at hand. Irish stew is a fine example of this. People have been known to add things like garlic to an Irish stew. Mother O'Reilly wouldn't know what garlic was and if she did she wouldn't care for it.

The non-negotiable ingredients of Irish stew are lamb, potatoes, and onions. The rest is optional. Carrots are good and feel free to pop in some leeks and celery if you have them. Americans, who think that lamb "tastes too strong", make their Irish stew with beef. You might as well make cheese fondue with Kraft slices.

I debate what is the best liquid to use for the stew. Some people say lamb stock. Lamb stock is good but as the lamb itself is going to give

a lot of taste to the sauce, I think lamb stock makes it too lamb-y. I have used Guinness. That's something Mother O'Reilly certainly has in her kitchen. Guinness, that umami-laden liquid, is good but you won't go far wrong just using water which is probably what most Irish peasant cooks used. The lamb will soon give it a strong taste. If you're reluctant to use Guinness, then use chicken stock which is a good compromise between water and something too strong tasting.

> "...People have been known to add things like garlic to an Irish stew. Mother O'Reilly wouldn't know what garlic was and if she did she wouldn't care for it."

Ingredients for four

+ 1kg neck fillet of lamb, diced into generous bite-size cubes; neck fillet with its marbling of fat is better than more expensive fillets like lamb loin whose lack of marbling will make them toughen up

+ 3 tbsp vegetable oil

+ 2 medium onions, sliced into half-moons

+ 750g medium to large potatoes (floury better than waxy) peeled and cut into slices the thickness of a pound coin

+ 2 celery sticks diced small (optional)

+ 2 large carrots diced

+ 1 tsp dried oregano

+ 1 tsp dried thyme (or 2 tsp fresh)

+ 750ml Guinness or chicken stock

+ Salt and pepper

What you do

Add the oil to a casserole dish with a lid and brown the lamb on all sides over medium-high heat for five minutes. Don't crowd the dish; you'll need to do it in batches. Add more oil if necessary. Reserve the lamb.

Add onions, celery and carrots and fry over medium-high heat for five minutes, splashing in some more oil if needed. Add the oregano and thyme and spread the lamb pieces over the top. Pour over the stout or stock and bring to the boil.

Reduce the heat to a simmer, give the stew a good grind of salt and pepper, and then spread the potato slices over the top, giving them another grind of salt and pepper. The potato slices should more than cover the whole stew while overlapping, sometimes two thick. Using the back of a wooden spoon press the potato slices down into the stock so they are just covered.

Put a lid on the casserole and slide into a 180c oven. Check after 1½ hours to see if the lamb is melt-in-the-mouth and the potatoes soft and unctuous with stock. Adjust seasoning if necessary. There should still be plenty of liquid but if it's looking dry and the potatoes are out of the liquid, add some water or stock. Turn the oven up to 200c or turn on the top grill and bang the stew back into the oven with no lid for five to ten minutes, just long enough to turn the potatoes brown.

I usually serve this in bowls with a spoon and a fork. You won't need a knife to cut the lamb and the spoon will allow you to scoop up the gravy. *Cabbage Is King (p.142)* goes well with this.

PERFICK PAELLA, NO, REALLY

What pizza is to Italy, paella is to Spain. Pizza started life as the cheapest food for the poorest people in southern Italy, a chunk of focaccia smeared with tomato and a splodge of olive oil. Now, in America and England, pizza has become a platform for pineapple, artichokes, chicken, coconut and, God save us, foie gras. Paella has been similarly traduced by us Anglos who consider it to be a seafood dish consisting of rice swimming in orange soup and topped with mussels, crab, prawns, lobster, and as many other bits of fish as you can fit on top. This is a dish unknown in Spain.

Paella, like gazpacho, is a peasant dish. When the Spanish finally kicked the Moors out in 1492, they kept the most precious gift the Moors had left behind in Spain. Rice. The Spanish love it. The finest rice in Spain comes from the region surrounding Valencia. It is a short grain rice called *bomba* and is similar to the great Italian risotto rices like *arborio* and *carnaroli*. *Bomba* has the ability to soak up even more liquid than they.

Rice was to Valencian peasants what potatoes were to the Irish, the food that kept them alive. Valencians lived on rice which they would cook with stock made from left-overs if they had them or just with paprika-flavoured water if they didn't. If they could find a few scraps of meat to throw on top, so much the better. The scraps were usually a bit of chicken, a rabbit caught in a nearby field, and a handful of easily found snails, somewhat smaller than the French escargots. Add lots of garlic and some paprika and there was your paella.

Paella, like cassoulet, another peasant dish that the further it gets from its peasant roots the less interesting it becomes, is named after the thing it is cooked in. A paella is a large, flat-bottomed pan. If you want to cook a decent paella, get a paella pan. They are not expensive. Don't use your thick-bottomed, expensive, stainless non-stick pan because you will not be able to produce a good *soccarat* in that, of which more later.

I love risotto and I love paella. In one respect they are similar. Both are all about the rice and the stock. You must have the right rice and you must have the best stock, preferably home-made. You cannot make risotto or paella with stock from a cube. No. A good risotto needs nothing apart from good stock, lots of butter, and maybe some chopped onion. Yes, you can add some porcini or zucchini if you want but they are optional extras. That's all a paella needs too, substituting oil for butter and adding lots of garlic and some paprika.

However, there is a major difference. Risotto, like scrambled eggs must be stirred continuously to develop its full creaminess. Paella must not be stirred at all. If you stir a paella you will never get a *soccarat*. *Soccarat* comes from the Spanish word for scorch. The perfect paella does not look like soup. In the perfect paella all the stock has been absorbed and the rice at the bottom has formed a wonderful gooey crust, similar to the sublime crust under Persian *chelo* rice.

The recipe below is for a meat-based paella. There's nothing wrong with fishy paellas. The whole idea of a paella, like a risotto, is that it should reflect whatever ingredients are available locally. However, don't think that by adding more and more ingredients you will get a better and better paella. The reverse is true. Remember, the heart of the paella is the rice, the stock and the soccarat. The rest is noise.

Ingredients for four

+ 300g *bomba* (or *arborio*) rice

+ 800ml chicken stock (not from a cube)

+ 4 garlic cloves, roughly chopped

+ 2 medium onions, chopped

+ 2 level tsp smoked paprika

+ 100ml fino sherry or dry white vermouth

+ 4 boneless chicken thighs, skin on

+ 15 cm piece of chorizo, roughly chopped

+ 3 red or yellow bell peppers chopped

+ 250g chopped tomatoes

+ Olive oil

+ Salt and pepper

What you do

It's not how the Spanish do it but I cook my rice and meat separately. That way you know the meat will be properly cooked. This recipe uses chicken thighs but use whatever meat you feel like. Small French-trimmed lamb chops are delicious and, when no Spaniards are looking, I sometimes grill some Cumberland sausages, slice them thickly and add them. The Spanish tried to garotte Jamie Oliver when he added chorizo to his paella so sliced Cumberland sausage could produce Hispano-apoplexy. Tastes good though.

Put the chicken, or whatever meat you are using, along with the bell peppers into a roasting tray. Sprinkle with olive oil and dried oregano. Cook for thirty minutes in a 200c oven. If you have a grill feature in your oven switch to that for the last five minutes to colour everything nicely. Take the chicken and peppers out and reserve.

Now it's time for the rice. First, warm the chicken stock in a saucepan and keep to hand. Then sweat the onions until translucent in your paella pan, add the tomatoes and garlic and sprinkle over the paprika. Some people add saffron. Go ahead if you like it. Turn the heat up and cook the mixture until it is starting to look sticky. Now add the rice and the sherry. Stir everything around to coat the rice. Add the warm chicken stock. Do it all in one go, unlike a risotto where you feed it in over time. Smooth out the rice so it is the same depth everywhere and then leave uncovered at a simmer until the liquid has been absorbed, probably twenty minutes more or less. Taste a little rice. It should be al dente, not soft but not chalky in the centre.

Soccarat time. Turn the heat right up. Do not stir. Listen carefully. After a minute or so you will hear a snap-crackle-pop from the rice. That is the rice at the bottom scorching to form a delicious crust.

Turn the heat to low, add the reserved chicken and peppers, tucking them well into the paella, cover with a cloth and leave to sit for ten minutes.

When you serve it be sure to make sure everyone scrapes up some *soccarat* from the bottom.

POT-ROAST
FENNEL CHICKEN

What is it about the words "pot" and "roast" that are so appealing? Restaurants love to lard their menus with redundant adjectives to make you think there is a peasant granny instead of a coke-snorting alcoholic in the kitchen. "Oven-baked" and "Pan-fried" are two restaurant weasel words. Dude, where else are you going to roast other than in an oven? A bath? And what is your alternative frying tool to a pan? A box? These words mean absolutely nothing. They are put there to arouse pleasant associations in your mind and to distract your attention from the fact that the restaurant's oven is in fact a microwave.

Pot-roast on the other hand means something. It means you have put your chicken or piece of beef or lamb in a heavy cast-iron pot on to which you have plopped a lid. You can then put it in an oven or on top of a stove. It's the pot that does the roasting however you apply the heat.

Before you pot-roast something you usually add some vegetables, seasonings, a bit of fat, and a bit of stock or booze. Unlike open or lidless roasting, which is great for many things, pot-roasting stops the liquids evaporating while the heat turns them into a delicious gravy. The flavour of the spices and herbs permeate everything. And, yes, it is how your granny used to cook and her granny before her except that her granny before her took the pot down to the village baker to shove in the back of his oven.

There's nothing glamorous or modern about pot-roasting. You will find few pot-roasts on Michelin-starred menus. But if you like traditional home cooking, it is unbeatable. There will be nothing left over.

Ingredients for four

+ 1 biggish chicken
+ Olive oil
+ Butter
+ 4 medium carrots, diced
+ 2 leeks cut into rounds
+ 2 sticks of celery, diced
+ 2 onions, peeled and quartered
+ 125g diced lardons
+ 2 butcher's sausages
+ 4 cloves of garlic left whole
+ 3 tsp fennel seeds
+ Salt and pepper
+ 200ml Madeira

What you do

Chop up your vegetables and keep them to hand. Don't worry if you don't have exactly the right veg or want to substitute, say, parsnip for the carrot, or shallots for the onion. Go ahead but please don't go putting anything acid or squashy like a tomato or an aubergine in. You don't want acid and you don't want to dilute the sauce.

Put your casserole dish, a heavy, high-sided, lidded one, on the hob on medium-high heat and add a splodge of olive oil and butter. Brown the chicken on all four sides.

Take the chicken out and add the vegetables, garlic, and lardons. Add the sausages if you are using them. Give everything a stir round and sprinkle half the fennel seeds and a good grind of salt and pepper over them. Plop the chicken, breast up, on top of the veg, and sprinkle the remaining fennel seeds over it.

Put this in a 200c oven with the lid on. If you don't have an oven, you could always cook this on top of the hob. It will take an hour to 1¼ hours to cook. Fifteen minutes before the end, take it out, check how it's doing by prising the thigh away from the body which should be only just pink, and add the Madeira by pouring it into the chicken's cavity and letting it leak out. Replace with no lid for another ten to fifteen minutes.

Take it out, let it rest with the lid on while you are eating your first course, then carve the chicken and slice each sausage into four or so bits. I usually put the carved chicken pieces in the middle of an oval serving plate, surround them with the vegetables, and then spoon juice over everything.

If you need starch you could serve this with mashed potatoes. I don't.

RED-EYE COQ

How I love the classic bistro dishes, leek vinaigrette, bavette a l'echalottes, boeuf bourguignon, moules marinieres, pot au feu, cassoulet, quenelles de brochet, soupe de poisson a la rouille, navarin d'agneau, choucroute garnie, and brandade de morue, to name the first ones that come to mind. Each one of these dishes, made with care and love, is as good as anything you could ever want to eat. But when did you last see them on a menu, even in France? The death of bistro cooking has been one of the sadnesses of modern life. I wonder if the French still make these dishes at home. I fear that the modern French housewife is keener on her microwave than her stock-pot.

Perhaps the classic dish is coq au vin. Yes, I remember in my twenties going to dinners given by three or four girls sharing a flat and more often than not the main course was a money-saving coq au vin or boeuf bourguignon, and more often than not, the thin weedy sauce, tough meat, and over-cooked vegetables made them inedible. But the true version of both dishes is ambrosial, particularly coq au vin.

Look in recipe books and you will see twenty recipes for coq au vin, all slightly different, but none of them is authentic because they all lack the essential ingredient of le vrai coq. Blood. The French peasant cook always added the blood of the coq to her dish, just as she would never cook civet de lièvre without adding the hare's blood. Blood gives a stew richness and depth. But if you don't kill your own coq, you're not going to get any blood with your butcher's free-range chicken.

So, a chap has to improvise. My Red-Eye Coq is a homage to coq au vin. It lacks the blood but has two added secret ingredients I never tell people about until they've finished mopping the sauce off their plate. You have to be careful. If you overdid either you would have a revolting dish but, in the right proportions, they give the same depth and richness to the dish that blood does.

You have all heard of red-eye gravy. It is a poor man's dish traditionally served with hot ham in the old Confederacy It is made from ham scratchings mixed with coffee. The red-eye name came from the fact that coffee can keep you awake. Red-eye gravy in the deep South is often greasy and unappealing, but whatever depth and character it has comes from the coffee. Coffee is one of my secret ingredients.

The other is molasses. I often use molasses in stews. It is like anchovies. Pounded-up salted anchovies give body and flavour to so many Italian dishes but you don't identify the anchovy taste in the finished dish, just its depth. Molasses, used sparingly, does the same. It adds that unique combination of bitterness and sweetness but once it disappears into the stew it just makes it richer.

"It lacks the blood but has two added secret ingredients I never tell people about until they've finished mopping the sauce off their plate."

126

Ingredients for four

+ 1 large chicken cut into eight pieces

+ 200g lardons

+ 10 small shallots or onions, peeled but kept whole

+ 2 medium carrots, diced

+ 1 stick of celery, diced

+ 200g button mushrooms, halved

+ 2 cloves garlic, finely chopped

+ Bottle of full-bodied fruity red wine (Southern Rhone or Languedoc is good)

+ ½ wine glass bourbon (calvados or brandy if you don't have bourbon)

+ 300ml chicken stock (not a cube)

+ 1 tbsp fresh thyme leaves

+ 2 level tsp instant coffee

+ 1 tbsp molasses

+ Flour, butter, olive oil

+ Four slices of sourdough bread toasted dry

What you do

Put a cupful of flour in a bag, drop in the chicken bits and shake them up. Take them out, shaking off the excess flour and brown them over medium heat in a big frying-pan in batches in a mixture of butter and olive oil. They should be gold, not black. Once browned, take them out and keep to the side. Briefly sauté the lardons, onions, carrot, celery, and garlic for a couple of minutes.

Take a big high-sided casserole dish. Put the chicken pieces in. Drain the fat off the other ingredients and add to the chicken. Add the bottle of wine, the bourbon, and the chicken stock. The liquid should easily cover the chicken. If it doesn't, add more wine or stock till the chicken is well covered. Bring to a gentle boil, and then lower heat to a simmer. Add the molasses and the instant coffee. Don't boil it or the chicken will get tough and the wine bitter. Put the lid on.

After twenty minutes, add the mushrooms and thyme. Season with salt and pepper. Keep simmering for another twenty minutes, take out a piece of chicken and cut open. If no pinkness remains, you're done. Taste the sauce and adjust the seasoning to your liking. Resist the temptation to go on tasting the sauce because it is so good.

Many people now take out the solids and reduce the sauce to make it thick and syrupy. I don't. I serve everything in a soup plate with plenty of sauce, soup-style. In addition to a knife and fork I give people a spoon for the sauce and the sourdough toast for dunking.

When they have finished mopping their plates, ask them if they can guess your two secret ingredients. No-one ever does.

SPANISH
PARTRIDGE

Some people don't like game. They find grouse, teal, and hare too dark and gamey. I love all three but I can understand that they are not to everyone's taste. For people who don't like the strong taste of game, there is an easy answer. Pheasant and partridge have the attraction of game, wild, not fatty, healthy, but at the same time not much stronger tasting than an old-fashioned chicken.

Not only are they healthy, they are amazing value and very easy to cook. In Norfolk I can buy a partridge for less than a Big Mac when they are in season. You can just pop your partridge or pheasant into a hot oven, roast it simply as a hundred recipe books will tell you how, and you have a fine dinner, particularly if you've made bread sauce.

For someone who likes the gamey taste, partridge can be a little bland which is why it's good to cook it in a way that adds flavour.

The world's greatest partridge shooters and eaters are the Spaniards. Their partridge shoots are the stuff of legend. On a traditional Spanish partridge shoot each gun will have two guns and a loader whose duty it is to pass the person shooting a freshly loaded gun immediately after they have fired. Each gun also has a *secretario*, an eagle-eyed old man with a notebook. If you miss an easy bird, he may suck his teeth, but if you bring one down, he will remember where each bird falls and when the drive is over he will hare off to collect your birds. In England, it is considered poor form to compare what you have shot with your neighbour's bag. In Spain it is de rigueur and if you don't do it, your *secretario* certainly will.

The Spanish have a hundred ways of cooking partridge. The one below is not an actual Spanish recipe but is my homage to Spanish partridge cookery. It would work as well with pheasant or even a poussin. The Mexicans, as we all know, love to use chocolate in their cooking. This love they passed on to the Spaniards. A little bit of chocolate, not unlike the molasses and coffee in my coq au vin, will add depth and savour to a sauce. We are not talking Cadbury's Dairy Milk here. Get some high quality, 70% or 85% cocoa, chocolate. It should be semi-bitter. The resulting dish is sublime...

Ingredients for two

+ 2 partridges
+ Good handful of lardons
+ Olive oil
+ 3 cloves of garlic, finely chopped
+ 2 carrots, diced
+ 1 medium onion, chopped
+ 2 tsp thyme
+ 500ml chicken stock
+ 100ml amontillado sherry
+ 100ml dark rum
+ Salt and pepper
+ 30g dark, 70% cocoa, chocolate

What you do

Put a splodge of olive oil in a large frying pan with a lid, throw in the lardons and brown the partridges on all sides over medium-high heat. Turn the heat down to medium and add the onions, garlic and carrots. Stir them around and cook for about seven minutes. Add the chicken stock, sherry, thyme, and rum. Season with salt and pepper. Cover the pan with a lid and cook at medium heat for about fifteen minutes. Check how cooked the partridge are by prising a leg from the body. It should be lightly pink on the inside, not bloody. Cook longer if necessary.

Lower heat, break the chocolate into small pieces and add. Give it a minute to melt and then stir. Taste and adjust seasoning. If you had to use sweet chocolate, you may need to add a squeeze of lemon to counteract the sweetness.

Take the partridge out of the pan, remove the legs and, using a sharp knife or game shears, cut the bird in half along the breast bone, and remove the back, leaving just the two breast halves along with the legs.

Put two breast halves and two legs in each plate and spoon the vegetable mixture and liquid over the top. Serve in soup bowls with lightly toasted sourdough for dunking.

"Not only are they healthy, they are amazing value and very easy to cook. In Norfolk I can buy a partridge for less than a Big Mac when they are in season."

SPEEDY MARINATED BUTTERFLIED LAMB

If you liked *Geraldine's Buggered Lamb (p.100)* you will like this, although in many ways it is the opposite. Geraldine's lamb cooks for five hours, this for twenty minutes. Geraldine's is made with cheap and fatty shoulder, this with expensive, lean, leg. Geraldine's is cooked until it is brown and falls off the bone, this until it's pink and ready to be carved into beautiful pink slices.

The thing the two recipes have in common is they both use the same delicious marinade.

Leg of lamb is one of the few things I seldom cook on the bone. I prefer butterfly-ing it. However, don't try to butterfly it yourself. You will make a hash of it. Ask your butcher to do it because he has the knowledge and the knives. When he's done it, you will have a piece of lamb which opens out to being around 45 cm long and 30 cm wide. It will be about 8 cm thick in the thickest part and half that in the thinnest. This is useful because, when cooked, the thick parts will be rare and the thin close to medium, thus allowing you to give people lamb cooked to their liking and not forcing everyone to have the same.

When it comes to the marinade, I've chosen the ingredients I like, but you should feel free to experiment and add or subtract to taste. Using different spices or substituting teriyaki sauce for my ketjaap manis, would be possible, for instance.

Ingredients for six

+ Butterflied leg of lamb (around 1.5kg after butterflying)

+ Salt and pepper

For the marinade

+ 6 salted anchovy fillets, chopped

+ 100ml ketjaap manis (Indonesian sweet soy-based sauce – if unavailable use teriyaki sauce)

+ Good dash of Worcester sauce

+ 1 tbsp dried thyme

+ 1 tbsp dried oregano

+ 2 tsp ground cloves

+ 2 tsp Chinese five spice powder

+ Juice of 1 lemon

+ 100ml dry white vermouth or fino sherry (dry white wine as a back-up)

+ 1 tbsp molasses

What you do

Put all the marinade ingredients in a bowl and mix them up well with a spoon. Taste the marinade and adjust for sweetness with brown sugar or lemon juice. Score the lamb on both sides with a sharp knife into a diamond pattern.

Put the lamb, underside up, in a big roasting tin. Spoon a tablespoon of marinade over it, rubbing it in with the back of the spoon. Repeat all over the underside until you've used almost half the marinade. Flip the lamb and repeat the process with the skin side using your spoon to work the rest of the marinade into the diamond scoring until you have used all the marinade. Some of the marinade will run off into the roasting pan. Don't worry about it. Leave the lamb in a cool place or the fridge for at least thirty minutes longer if you have the time.

Heat the oven to 240c. This should be done in a very hot oven. Note that this will cook in far less time than it takes to cook a bone-in leg.

Take the leg out of the fridge half an hour before cooking to allow it to warm to room temperature and give it a good grind of salt and pepper on the upper, skin, side. Slide into the middle of the very hot oven. After fifteen minutes take it out and test for doneness by cutting into the thickest part. If it is blue in the middle, put it back for another five minutes, remembering that it will cook a bit more after you have taken it out. When ready, take it out and let it rest under a cloth while you eat your first course.

Put the lamb on a board for carving. The run-off marinade and lamb juices will have formed a delicious gravy. Pour this into a jug and serve with the lamb. Unlike a bone-in leg of lamb, this is a doddle to carve. Cut it into slices 1 cm thick and serve. A simple green vegetable and new potatoes go well. So does my *Mint Relish (p.170)*.

STICKY-FINGERS QUAIL

Quail was once a wild bird in England. It still is in much of America and parts of Europe and Asia but is now rare in England. These days it is farmed. It's easy to buy farmed quail at a good butcher or online. There are lots of excellent suppliers. The problem with farmed quail is the birds don't any longer have the wild-bird taste of, say, a grouse or wild duck. That means that when you cook it you need to cook it in a way that adds taste to the little bird. If you are cooking, for instance, a grouse or a teal, you would be mad to add things to it because the gamey taste is already in the bird itself. The opposite is true with quail.

Don't turn your nose up at quail. The recipe below is one of the best get-the-party-going starters for a dinner. Or serve it with a big green salad as a summer main course. There is something about people using their fingers to eat that both makes the food taste better and puts everyone in a good mood. No one can be pompous or formal while smearing their face with sticky-fingers quail.

> "Don't turn your nose up at quail. The recipe below is one of the best get-the-party-going starters for a dinner."

Ingredients for four to six (depending on whether it is a starter or main course)

+ 8 quail, or even 12, if people are hungry. There is not a lot of meat on a quail.

+ Pepper and salt

For the marinade/glaze

+ 150ml dark soy sauce

+ 150ml ketjaap manis (substitute teriyaki sauce if you don't have it)

+ 150ml medium Madeira (Duke of Clarence is good)

+ 2 tbsp molasses

+ 1 tbsp Worcester sauce

+ 1 tsp five-spice powder

+ 1 tbsp Dijon mustard or Patak's aubergine pickle (the latter is spicier)

+ Salt

What you do

First, make the marinade by mixing together all the ingredients in a bowl. Then pour the marinade into a big Ziploc or similar bag.

You now need to spatchcock the quail. With a knife, or better with game shears, cut out the backbone and discard leaving you with butterflied birds. Put the birds in the marinade bag, close it, and give the bag a good shake to make sure that all parts of all the birds are in contact with the marinade. Leave it for at least half an hour in the fridge. Longer would be better though I doubt you would taste the difference.

Turn your grill up to very hot. Cover a baking tray with foil. Take the quail out of the marinade bag and shake most but not all of the marinade back into the bag. Lay the quail out, skin side up and as flat as possible on the foil. You will probably need to cook the quail in at least two batches but don't worry, they will be happy keeping warm in the warming drawer.

Slide the tray in close to the grill, best would be a hand's breadth below it. Leave the birds to grill for three to five minutes depending on the heat of your grill. You want the edges starting to blacken but you don't want the bird black and scorched. Take them out, flip them over on to the non-skin side, spread them out well, and pop back under the grill for another two minutes to give the underside a touch of colour.

Take them out and cut one of the birds in half down the middle. Inspect. The flesh by now should be white, not pink. If it's pink, put them back for another minute or two. When they are all cooked, cut each bird in half and slide a knife between the legs and the breast to remove the legs, turning each quail into four pieces. Mound all the pieces in a large bowl and keep warm.

Meanwhile pour the marinade into a saucepan, bring to the boil, stir a couple of times, taste and adjust the balance, then pour the marinade into a jug.

Serve by putting the quail bowl in the middle of the table inviting people to help themselves. If possible, give everyone a little individual bowl into which you pour some of the hot marinade for them to use as a dipping sauce. Hand out knives and forks for the salad but you really have to eat the quail with your sticky fingers.

TOAD IN NO HOLE

There are certain things that visitors to England pretend to like to show how English they are, in much the same way that English expatriates in New York pretend to like Reuben sandwiches and the disgusting mustard Americans put on their hot dogs. On the list of sacred English food are kippers, Cooper's Oxford Marmalade, potted shrimps, spotted dick and custard, ripe game, jugged hare, jellied eels, trifle, and of course Toad in the Hole. To be fair, once foreigners can be persuaded to try Toad, everyone likes it, it's just the name that makes visitors think they are being daring by eating it.

Toad isn't that old a dish when compared with, say, jugged hare or steak and kidney pie, although versions of it must have been around for ever before it acquired its majestic name, just as people had been eating grilled cheese on toast for centuries before anyone thought to call it Welsh rarebit. The original Toad was made with left-over meat submerged in batter and cooked. Way-back-when, people used to make more use of left-overs than they do today. As a result, left-over meat crept quietly away to be replaced by Toads of juicy English pork sausages.

There is a problem though. The other thing that has changed has been people's tolerance for stodge, once the cornerstone of the British diet. Stodge can be delicious and few things more delicious than a well-risen, airy, duvet of crisp batter enveloping the sausages particularly when bathed in onion gravy. If you want to make proper Toad, Nigel Slater and others have great recipes for that. You don't need me to tell you how.

My No-Hole Toad has as much stodge as my *No Bread Summer Pudding (p.163)*. That's none. It's for those times you don't want a duvet of batter. My toads are hiding in a welter of roast vegetables. Few things are better than roast vegetables. The miracle of applying consistent heat to a vegetable is that acidity and astringency convert themselves into caramelly sweetness.

Nothing could be simpler and less trouble than Toad in No Hole. If you don't have, or don't like, the selection of vegetables I have below, substitute the ones you do like. As long as they are roastable they'll be as good. And if you are craving carbs I suppose you could chop up a potato or two and add them but they won't make it taste better and you'll feel better if you don't.

> "On the list of sacred English food are kippers, Cooper's Oxford Marmalade, potted shrimps, spotted dick and custard, ripe game, jugged hare, jellied eels, trifle, and of course Toad in the Hole."

Ingredients for two greedy people

+ 6 traditional English sausages, like Cumberland or Lincoln

+ 100g lardons

+ 4 cloves of garlic, topped and tailed

Use all or a selection of the vegetables below and feel free to add things like broccoli, halved Brussel sprouts, or a sprinkle of kale. I'd avoid courgette and aubergine as too mushy.

+ 3 onions, peeled and chopped into wedges

+ 4 bell peppers, de-seeded, de-pithed and sliced

+ 2 medium carrots, diced

+ 2 banana shallots, halved into "boats" with outer skin removed

+ Handful of cherry tomatoes

+ 1 tbsp dried thyme

+ Olive oil

+ Salt and pepper

What you do

Put a heavy-bottomed frying pan on a medium-low heat, add a small splodge of oil, followed by the sausages. While the vegetables are roasting you will slowly fry the sausages, turning them occasionally so they brown on all sides. You could cook the sausages with the vegetables but they would be less juicy and lack the wonderful caramel effect you will get from slow frying. The sausages, cooked slowly, will take half an hour. Remove the pan from the heat and leave the sausages to keep warm.

While the sausages are cooking, take a big roasting pan. Line it with foil if you want to avoid heavy washing up later. Spread your chopped vegetables over the pan. Sprinkle the lardons over them. You should have enough veg so they cover the bottom but are not overlapping too much. Sprinkle a generous glug of olive oil over everything, a good grind of pepper and lots of salt. Stir the veg around to make sure everything is coated in oil. Scatter the dried thyme over everything.

Put this in the middle of a 200c oven. After twenty minutes take the pan out and stir the veg. After another twenty minutes, take the pan out and taste a little bit of onion and pepper. By now they should be soft and sweet. If your oven has a top grill, I like to switch from roast mode to grill for the last five minutes. This will give everything a charred edge but keep a careful eye on the pan as you don't want charcoal vegetables.

Take the vegetables out and spread over an oval serving platter. Hide the sausages in the vegetables. Serve on warm plates. This doesn't need side dishes but Dijon mustard, Worcester sauce, or a good chutney are nice accompaniments.

TREACLY HAM WITH MARMALADE SAUCE

What is easy to cook, loved by everyone, perfect for feeding lots of people, easy to serve, and provides delicious leftovers for days to come? If you didn't say ham, it's time you did. Cooking ham is a doddle. It's also virtually fool proof. If you're cooking beef and lamb you have to get the right degree of doneness. Can be tricky. Ham on the other hand is tolerant. It's difficult to cook ham badly.

People can be put off cooking ham because they are told to soak it in fresh water to remove the salt. We've moved on. These days the ham or gammon you buy is unlikely to be salty enough to need soaking in advance. As you will be buying your ham from your excellent butcher, not Sainsbury's, check with him if it needs rinsing first.

People are also confused about the difference between ham and gammon. Ain't none. They're all bits of pig that have been cured with salt, either with brine or dry-cured. Technically speaking gammon and ham are from the hind leg of a pig but you can find lots of cuts in the butcher, often rolled and tied like a shoulder of lamb, which call themselves gammon and very good they are too. The only difference is that gammon is raw and needs cooking while ham is already cooked although it'll be much better if you put a glaze on it and cook it some more to finish it.

This recipe is for gammon but feel free to use the last part of this recipe, the glazing and roasting process, for a bought ham as well. One important shopping tip. Buy a piece of gammon that has lots of fat on it. This is what's going to be covered with most of the glaze and is everyone's favourite bit. Thanks to the health fascists, modern pigs can be disgracefully lean. You don't want that.

You can of course buy a gammon "steak" but I wouldn't. Once cooked, it will be dry and stringy. Leave that to our American friends who will serve it up with a slice of pineapple and possibly a glacé cherry on top.

I would suggest you get a gammon piece weighing at least half a kilo and preferably well over a kilo. If you have lots of people, or it's Christmas, get a two or three kilo gammon. As a rule of thumb, one kilo will feed four people with enough over to make delicious ham sandwiches or chunks to go in pea soup. The gammon you buy should have the rind on it.

Most recipes will tell you to add herbs and spices to the cooking water for the gammon. I don't as I'm not going to make a stock from it.

The marmalade sauce is something I invented as I love Cooper's Original Oxford marmalade. If you don't have Cooper's, use another thick marmalade with some bitterness. It's possibly the simplest-to-make sauce ever but it's good. I'm told that people under forty don't eat marmalade. Theirs is the loss.

"I'm told that people under forty don't eat marmalade. Theirs is the loss."

Ingredients for four

+ 1kg smoked boneless gammon with rind (unsmoked is fine too; as a rule smoked will taste a bit saltier, unsmoked a bit blander). This recipe works fine for a turkey-sized four or five kilo ham.

For the glaze

+ 2 tbsp Dijon mustard

+ 3 tbsp honey

+ 3 tbsp molasses

For the marmalade sauce

+ 200g Cooper's Original Oxford marmalade. The marmalade must be thick, dark, and slightly bitter. Substitute at your peril.

+ 200ml Madeira (Duke of Clarence) or sweet sherry (Harvey's Bristol Cream)

+ Knob of butter

What you do

You can boil your gammon or you can bake it. The cooking time is the same. You cook it for 20 minutes per 500g plus 20 minutes. In other words, a 1kg gammon will take an hour and twenty minutes to cook, 2kg will take an hour and forty minutes. My advice is to boil it first and then bake it, splitting the cooking time equally between them.

If you're doing that, first plop the gammon into a large saucepan, fill it with enough water to cover the gammon, put on a lid, bring to a slow boil and simmer for forty minutes. Remove the gammon and put on a board. When cool enough to handle get a sharp knife and remove the skin while leaving on as much fat as possible. Make right-angled diagonal slashes in the fat leaving yourself with diamonds cut in the fat. Apply the glaze all over the fat with the back of a spoon, trying to get as much as possible into the cuts in the fat. Use whatever is left to cover the rest of the joint.

Line a baking tin with foil, place the ham in the middle and put into the middle of a 200c oven for forty minutes. Halfway through take the ham out and spoon the glaze over the top.

Take the ham out and let it rest. Check the internal temperature if you have a thermometer. If it's over 60c, it's cooked.

While the ham is cooking you can make the marmalade sauce. Put the ingredients into a small saucepan over a medium heat. Mash the marmalade up with a fork to get rid of the chunks, simmer gently for five minutes and taste. If it's too sweet, add some lemon juice. If it's too tart, add some honey. Ideally it should have a slight bitter edge to it.

When you take the ham out of the roasting tin to put it on a carving platter to rest, you will see a pool of liquid glaze in the bottom of the pan along with some black gunge. Pour the liquid part into the marmalade sauce. It will make it taste even better. People have been known to eat the black gunge with a teaspoon while no-one is looking. I couldn't possibly comment.

Opinions differ as to how to carve a gammon. I think that ham, like smoked salmon, should be carved into thin slices, not quite see-through like salmon, but almost. Germans, the world's greatest pork-eaters, serve their ham in doorsteps. That's their privilege but I wouldn't follow them.

I accompany the gammon with *Lumpy Potatoes (p.147)* and *Cabbage Is King (p.142)*.

Vegetables

BUTTERY
LEEKS

Buddhist monks don't eat leeks because they
"excite the senses". Who knew? I love leeks
but I can't say my senses get excited by them.
There is something comforting about a leek;
you don't find leeks prancing around much
in posh restaurants. You probably already
have your favourite leek recipes but here
is a very simple one to add to them. This is
a wonderful but substantial vegetable to
accompany something light. But it's also a
terrific starter in its own right.

"Buddhist monks don't eat leeks because they "excite the senses". Who knew?"

Ingredients for four

+ 1kg leeks, white edible bit only
+ Big splodge of butter
+ 150g lardons
+ Splash of dry sherry or white vermouth
+ Salt and pepper

What you do

Cut the leeks into pieces about 2cm long. For some reason, they look nicer if you cut them on the diagonal. Put a large frying pan on medium heat and add the splodge of butter, followed by the leeks, lardons and sherry. Move the leeks around to make sure they are well-coated with butter. Put a lid on the pan, give them a stir halfway through, and in about fifteen minutes they will be ready. Lots of salt and pepper and serve on warm plate.

CABBAGE IS KING

Let's face it. Cabbage is not posh. Broccoli is posh. Kale is posh. So are artichokes and endives, celeriac and salsify, tofu and quinoa, but not cabbage. Go to a "fine dining" establishment (what a dreadful expression is "fine dining", I can feel little fingers crooking at the mention of it) and you will find celeriac and salsify and the rest of them dancing their way across the twelve course Tasting Menu but poor Jack Cabbage is nowhere to be seen. He is all the better for that.

What did the ancient Celts, Normans, pharaonic Egyptians, Diogenes, the Emperor Augustus, Babylonians, Charlemagne, Peter the Great, and Genghis Khan have in common? Clue - it was not a liking for quinoa. They loved cabbage. You can eat it raw in a salad, pickle it, turn it into sauerkraut or kimchi, steam it, stuff it and stew it, braise it or fry it, and whatever you do it will have a happy smile on its face, as will you. The only thing you mustn't do is cook it English boarding-house style by boiling it for half an hour.

Did you know that the ship's doctor on Captain Cook's ship that sailed in 1769 took plenty of cabbage along because it warded off scurvy? He also used sauerkraut to prevent gangrene. I have to admit that lots of people are not crazy about sauerkraut. It seems the same applies to the gangrene bacteria.

I love cabbage. It is my go-to vegetable. Health freaks are always lecturing me on how I must eat spinach and kale because they are packed with vital vitamins. They can keep their spinach and kale, but Mr Cabbage delivers more vitamins than Boots the Chemist. Ask Captain Cook's doctor. You didn't find him filling his galley with kale.

Cabbage is delicious, a veg for all seasons, the Labrador of veg cooking.

Here's a simple way of cooking it which takes but a few minutes. If you are eating it as a supper dish by itself, and a very good supper it makes, put the sausages in. If you want it as a vegetable to accompany a roast, leave the sausages out and put the bacon in.

There are two ways to make this dish depending on how you are going to be serving it. The first is the way described below. This is perfect when the cabbage is a supporting vegetable or when, with sausages, it is a complete supper dish. If, however, you want to use the cabbage centre stage, rather than as a supporting vegetable, such as when you might cover a serving plate with cabbage and then put bits of roast pheasant dotted about on top, then you want shredded cabbage. See alternative instruction below.

Ingredients for four

+ 1 cabbage, savoy (best), green, or white, not red or Chinese, de-cored and chopped into postage stamp-size pieces

+ [For shredded cabbage (see text above) – slice the cabbage into quarters, remove the hard core and then shred the cabbage by slicing down the sides of the quarters]

+ 1 large yellow onion or 2 small ones, sliced thin rather than chopped

+ 1 big or two small crisp apples, skin on, thinly sliced

+ 4 good English butcher's sausages or 5 rashers of streaky bacon, chopped (see last paragraph above)

+ 15 crushed juniper berries

+ Good sprinkle of caraway seeds

+ Splash of dry white vermouth, fino sherry, or light stock

+ Olive oil

+ Pepper and salt – a lot

+ Optional: knob of butter

What you do

First, put your sausages (if you are using them) on to cook. You can grill, fry, or bake them. When cooked, keep warm.

Sauté the onion and apple in olive oil over medium heat in a wok or big pan until the onion is soft but not brown. If you're not using sausages, put the chopped bacon in now with the onion and apples. Add the other ingredients, except the vermouth / sherry. Let everything cook over medium-high heat for three minutes or so. Add the alcohol and turn the heat up to high. Cook for a further two minutes. The alcohol should evaporate. Taste a piece of cabbage for seasoning and to make sure it is done. It should be al dente, neither crisp nor soft.

Cut the reserved sausages into rounds and stir into the cabbage. Serve it up, adding, if you're in the mood, a large knob of butter when you do.

CRASH POTATOES

These are delicious. I know one man who can hardly locate his own kitchen, cannot make toast, and leaves all the cooking to his wife. He thinks Crash Potatoes are so good that he sniffs his way to the kitchen, elbows his long-suffering wife from the stove, and makes the Crash Potatoes himself.

I'd like to say I invented them. I didn't but I can't remember who I stole the recipe from. The recipes all tell you to use olive oil. That's good, but I prefer butter. If you Google them you will find that most of the population of Australia claims to have invented them. G'day guys, good on yer, and thanks for bonzer spuds.

Ingredients for four

+ 8 waxy new potatoes
+ 8 knobs of butter or 3 tablespoons olive oil
+ Lots of salt and pepper
+ Rosemary or your other favourite herb, fresh and chopped

What you do

Cook the potatoes as normal in boiling water but take them out while they still have some bite in them.

Cover a roasting pan with a sheet of foil. Dry the spuds and put them on the foil with room between them. Get your potato masher out and give the spuds a squodge down so they spread out a little with parts of the skin split. You don't want to flatten them. They should be little mounds. You may need to use a fork to separate the squashed spuds from the masher. Flick any bits that have stuck to the masher back on to the spud.

Now you have a choice. Olive oil or butter? Either put a big knob of butter on each squodged spud or sprinkle then with olive oil. Olive oil is crisper; butter is, well, butterier. They're both terrific. Grind on lots of salt and pepper, plus a bit of chopped rosemary or thyme or whatever.

Pop in the top of a 200c oven until they are looking toasty on top, about 20 minutes. Slide a spatula underneath them and serve. They go brilliantly with lamb but are also good with everything else.

LUMPY POTATOES

These are so called because grand-daughter Elsa, then age 7, once said, "Grandad, your potatoes are lumpy." "Oh," said I, "Well you don't have to eat them." "No, they're delicious." A woman of discerning taste is Elsa. Mashed potatoes are a personal thing. The French like pomme purée. They are welcome to it. It's fine if you have lost your teeth and enjoy mush. I have even heard that Americans have been known to make mashed potatoes with olive oil. No thank you. I like my mashed potatoes to taste of butter and to put up a fight, not slither down my throat.

Cookery writers tell you to use floury potatoes that will make light, fluffy mashed potatoes. That's fine if you're after something light and fluffy with no potato taste. I'm not. I'm after butch spuds with lots of spud taste. I use waxy new potatoes such as the French ratte or Charlotte potatoes or anything else with nice yellow flesh.

Ingredients for four

+ 1kg Charlotte or similar potatoes (unpeeled for more potato taste)

+ 5 spring onions, chopped into small bits

+ 100ml milk

+ Giant splodge of butter

+ Lots of salt and pepper

What you do

Cut the potatoes into smallish cubes. Put them in boiling water for 10 to 15 minutes until they are softening but still have a bit of firmness in the middle. Drain thoroughly. Put back on the hob and shake them around for half a minute to dry them off completely. Take off the heat and add the milk. Using a potato masher, mash them till they are almost smooth but still have a few lumps. Don't worry about the bits of skin. Throw in the diced spring onions which will soften with the heat of the potatoes. Add the giant splodge of butter, the more you add the better it will taste, together with twice the amount of salt and pepper you think you need. Use a fork to stir the melting butter into the mix. Taste for seasoning and serve.

ENDIVE, QUEEN OF THE DARK

A chance remark from my supercook friend Phyllida, Queen of the Sunday lunch, got me thinking about endive so I Googled it. I found out a lot of stuff I didn't know. Who knew that endive, radicchio, escarole and frisée are all the same animal? You probably did but I didn't. Have a Google yourself, not of the recipes but the vegetable. It's fascinating. And the things those clever Belgians do to the endive to make it grow. It's the kind of thing I thought went out with Abu Ghraib. Darkness, deprivation, forcing. Everything but waterboarding.

Below though is a sweet and fitting end to a vegetable that has survived the indignities to which the Belgians have subjected it.

People are always adding sugar or honey to endives to "counteract the bitterness". That's because they cook them for fifteen minutes on the stove top, not long enough to lose their bitterness. Endives are like onions. They need long cooking, not honey or sugar, to lose their astringency and become naturally sweet.

These roast endives make a perfect complement to roast lamb or chicken. Or a pork chop. Or a roast pheasant.

Ingredients for four

+ Six endives (four if you are serving lots of other vegetables)

+ Lots of butter (and, please, don't go substituting olive oil for the butter. Olive oil is great but it doesn't have the taste of butter. You need that here.)

What you do

Cut the endives in half lengthwise and discard any dodgy outer leaves, creating twelve endive "boats". Put them in an oven dish big enough so they are not touching. Dob a couple of sugarlump sized knobs of butter on top of each boat. Bung them in a 200c oven, probably along with your roast. Cook them for at least 45 minutes or until they are soft, brown and steeped in caramelly butter. Give them a good grind of pepper and salt. Serve with the roast.

Or, if you want to have them by themselves for a simple Sunday supper, be my guest.

HALFWAY-TO-MARRAKECH VEGETABLES

I have not called these Moroccan vegetables because some Moroccan cooking pedant will pipe up that "Moroccans would never do that" or "Moroccan vegetables always have this".

I love Moroccan food but am no expert in Moroccan cookery as the Moroccans do it so much better than I ever could. However, there is no reason why you and I can't chop up some vegetables, add some liquid, throw in dried fruit and a few of our favourite spices and come up with a truly delicious dish. That's what I hope I have done. If it reminds you of Marrakech, so much the better, but please don't tell me I've left out the preserved lemon, the harissa, or the saffron.

The other great bonus of this dish is that it goes so well with so many things. Splodge a heap of Halfway-to-Marrakech Vegetables next to roast lamb or chicken, underneath a juicy pork chop, or on the side of beef short ribs and you will have an epic meal. This dish will keep for a few days in the fridge, with the flavours deepening every day. Eat it cold out of the fridge for lunch by itself with a glass of rosé sitting in your garden or, if you do what I do, make three times as much as you need, and you will find that the extra freezes brilliantly.

And, please, don't panic at the long list of ingredients. You will find this is one of the simplest things to cook.

Ingredients for six

I suggest you use the ingredients below as a suggestions list. If you follow it exactly you will get a great dish but if you want to, for instance, put in more root veg because it's winter, pop in some parsnips or turnips. Likewise, if you don't have dried apricots or raisins, use prunes or dates. Play around with the spices as much as you like. You're the person who's going to be eating it. You could even add preserved lemon if you insisted…

+ Big splodge of olive oil
+ 3 onions chopped into narrow wedges
+ 4 red or yellow bell peppers, de-seeded and sliced
+ 6 garlic cloves, squashed and chopped
+ 1 big, or 2 small, thumbs of ginger, diced fine
+ 1 tbsp ground cumin
+ 1 tbsp ground coriander
+ 1 tbsp five spice powder
+ 1 tsp chilli flakes
+ 2 sticks of cinnamon
+ 15 cardamom pods, squashed with the flat of a knife
+ 6 anchovy fillets, chopped
+ 1 big (or 2 small) aubergines
+ 2 courgettes, diced
+ 600g (1½) cans of chopped tomatoes
+ 500ml chicken or vegetable stock (or water if you don't have stock but not a cube)
+ 300g dried apricots, chopped
+ 200g raisins
+ 400g can of chickpeas, drained
+ 100g almond flakes, toasted in a pan
+ Juice of 1 lemon (optional)
+ 1 tbsp honey (optional)
+ Salt and pepper
+ Bunch of fresh coriander chopped

What you do

Put a big, deep, cast-iron casserole or similar over medium heat. Put in the onions and olive oil, sauté till soft. Then add the bell peppers, the garlic, the anchovies, and all the spices. Stir for a few minutes to let the spices create a fragrance. Now put in the aubergine and courgettes. Stir so that they are well coated in spices and add the tomatoes and stock. Turn the heat up to medium-high for five minutes or so while stirring well. Throw in the apricots and raisins. Give a good grind of salt and pepper.

Turn the heat down to a simmer and leave the mixture for forty minutes, stirring occasionally. The liquid should reduce to an almost sticky consistency. Put the lid on if it's reducing too quickly and turn the heat up a bit if it's too liquid.

Taste the vegetables, they should be meltingly soft by now. If not, cook a little more.

Finally, add the toasted almonds and the drained chickpeas. Taste. If too acid, add the honey; if too sweet, add the lemon juice.

Before serving, sprinkle the chopped coriander on top and stir.

This dish is best served warm rather than hot. It is excellent cold. A night or two in the fridge will only make it taste better.

MILO
BAYILDI

Everyone knows the wonderful Turkish aubergine dish, Imam Bayildi, which literally means "the imam swooned", because the imam thought it was so good. Well, this is a different dish but equally faintworthy. Pass the smelling salts. It is a terrific starter or it goes well as an accompaniment to summer food. I like it with roast chicken, served warm (the chicken, not the aubergine which should be cool).

Ingredients for four

+ 500g aubergines, sliced lengthwise into 1cm thick strips, skin on

+ 100ml olive oil

+ 6 handfuls of mint

+ 8 inches of cucumber, de-seeded and chopped

+ 1 handful finely-chopped spring onions

+ 1 teaspoon ground ginger or two teaspoons chopped fresh ginger

+ 400ml Greek yoghurt

+ 1 tbsp horseradish sauce

+ 1 tbsp honey

+ Juice of 2 limes

+ Teaspoon of chilli flakes

+ [Optional: chopped walnuts, pistachios, or pomegranate seeds]

+ Salt and pepper

What you do

Grill the sliced aubergines on a medium-hot griddle till they are soft and have nice griddle marks on both sides. It will take ten to fifteen minutes depending on thickness and heat. When they are done put the olive oil in a shallow bowl, add salt and pepper and drench each aubergine slices in the oil. Take out and reserve on a plate.

Destalk the mint and chop very finely. Put in a bowl with the chopped cucumber and spring onions and the other ingredients. Mix well with a spoon. Taste and add some salt.

Spread the yoghurt-mint mixture on a serving plate, place the aubergine slices on top, drizzle a bit of oil over and a crack of pepper and serve. Before serving I like to sprinkle over it some chopped walnuts or pistachios, or some pomegranate pips, just one of these, not all three.

Desserts

DAD'S MANGO KULFI

I can't remember where this recipe came from. I certainly didn't make it up myself. I have a feeling it came out of the New York Times some time in the 1970s. Kulfi, as those of you who have been to India know, is Indian ice cream. It has a particularly delicious fudge-like quality. This is because it is properly made with full cream milk that has been greatly reduced. The trouble with reducing milk is that it takes so long because it boils over if you get impatient. Never fear. For the impatient Western cook, aka me, help is at hand. That nice Mr Nestle has done the job for you and will sell you a can of excellent ready reduced milk. It's called condensed milk and what a wonderful product it is.

Mango kulfi has been a part of our family Christmas Eves since the days in the mid-1970s when we lived in Westchester, fifty miles north of New York.

"For the impatient Western cook, aka me, help is at hand. That nice Mr Nestle has done the job for you and will sell you a can of excellent ready reduced milk. It's called condensed milk and what a wonderful product it is."

Ingredients for four

+ Two cans of frozen mango slices in syrup

+ One can of condensed milk

+ Juice of three limes

+ ½ cup of double cream

+ Nutmeg

What you do

Take both ends off the frozen mango cans by holding them under hot water for a bit, removing top and bottom with a tin-opener and pushing out two frozen cylinders of mango and syrup. Chop roughly into chunks. Put chunks in the Magimix. Add a can of condensed milk. Add the juice of 3 to 4 limes. Add half a cup of cream. Grate nutmeg into mixture.

Turn on Magimix and pulse till mixture is frozen slush. Don't do it too much so it goes liquid. Just enough to eliminate any frozen chunks of mango.

Put the slush in a food container in the freezer and turn over every hour to prevent it freezing into a block. It's best made the same day as overnight in the freezer will freeze it solid.

Spoon into bowls and grate a bit more nutmeg on top when you serve.

On second thoughts, make double the quantities above because I guarantee you will want some on Christmas evening.

DRUNKEN WINTER
FRUIT SALAD

I don't do puddings. Puddings are usually full
of much-too-delicious things like cream and
sugar and I'm fat enough already. Or they're
cake or little pies that have to be baked.
I don't do baking. You have to measure
the ingredients and get the
temperatures right.
Not for me. Trubbliz
people expect something
when they have
finished their main
course. Here's one
people love.

Ingredients for four

+ A couple of handfuls each of dried apricots and figs (try to get the apricot-colour apricots, not the dark brown ones – looks more appetising).

+ A couple of handfuls of raisins or "mixed vine fruits"

+ Two oranges, peeled and chopped into smallish pieces

+ Wineglass (175ml) bourbon whiskey and / or rum

+ Couple of shots of elderflower cordial

+ 150ml apple juice

+ Cinnamon

+ Nutmeg

What you do

Take the zest off the oranges with a peeler and slice and dice into small strips. Chop the dried fruit into halves. Put them and the raisins in a saucepan. Add a wineglass of bourbon and a shot of cordial. Rum is good if you don't have bourbon and if you don't have elderflower cordial, perhaps a dash of Cointreau. Add enough water to cover the fruits. Add a flat teaspoon of ground cinnamon or a stick of cinnamon and of ground nutmeg. Bring to boil, turn heat down and simmer for half an hour, adding a bit more water if the fruit is drying out. Five minutes before the end add the apple juice and oranges. Remove from heat. Add the orange zest and mix. Taste. It should be sweet and syrupy. If it's not you can add a spoon of honey. If it's too sweet, squeeze some lemon in.

Let the fruit salad cool, then put it in the fridge.

Serve with dollops of crème fraiche. You could serve with a wodge of vanilla ice-cream. I don't.

GREENGAGE COMPOTE

People think of compotes as nursery puddings.
I love nursery puddings. True, a compote lacks
the panache of a pavlova but if you have ripe
summer fruits all you want is something to let
the fruit stand in the centre of the stage without
unnecessary trimmings. Few things do that
better than this greengage compote. Mirabelles
and Victoria plums also make wonderful
compotes. All three have a perfect balance of
tartness and sweetness which goes perfectly
with the crème fraiche.

Ingredients for four to six

+ 750g very ripe greengages

+ 150ml water

+ 100ml chestnut honey (you need a
  thick honey with real flavour, not just
  sweetness)

+ 1 lemon halved

+ 2 cinnamon sticks

+ 1 nutmeg to grate

+ Crème fraiche – to serve

What you do

Cut the greengages in half and remove
the stones. Boil the water in a kettle. Put
all the ingredients except the nutmeg in
a saucepan on a low to medium heat and
pour the boiling water over them. When
the honey has melted, taste the mixture
for sweetness and adjust by adding more
honey or a little lemon juice. Simmer, with
occasional stirring, for between five to
ten minutes depending on how ripe your
greengages are.

When the greengages are ready to collapse,
take the pan off the heat and pour the
compote into a bowl to cool; then put it in
the fridge.

This is best served in individual bowls with
a quick grate of nutmeg and a big blob of
cold crème fraiche.

MUM'S GREENGAGE FOOL

One summer in Norfolk a friend with a greengage tree made me a present of two big bags of greengages. Greengages take me back to being a ten-year-old, climbing the greengage tree in the bottom of our neighbour's garden to pick the fruits which had ripened from a chilly green to a voluptuous yellow-gold and were oozing droplets of syrup. This was a hazardous venture as there is nothing a wasp likes more than greengages oozing syrup. It was made doubly hazardous by the neighbour, Mrs Wombwell, coming out and shaking her walking stick at us: "Mrs Morland, your boys is stealing my greengages again."

Since then I have come across greengages rarely. They have a short season and restaurants never serve them. Presented with this tide of greengages I had to decide what to do with them. Ripe greengages don't last long. The first thing was easy. My mother used to make a wonderful greengage fool, that quintessential English dessert. Second, why not a greengage compote, another traditional English dessert? And then I stumbled on a recipe for Damson Gin. Eureka. I had greengages, not damsons, and I don't like gin, so I would do Greengage Vodka. I did, and modesty forbids I should say how good it was. Oh, OK. Someone sitting round my table after dinner said it was the best after-dinner drink they had ever had. I couldn't disagree with them.

You don't have to use greengages. I love them but the tiny French mirabelles are even better while the English Victoria plum with its tartness makes a fantastic compote.

The recipes for Mum's Greengage Fool and the Greengage Compote are here. You'll find the recipe for **Greengage Vodka (p.174)** elsewhere. Do all three.

Ingredients for four

+ 500g greengages
+ 1 tbsp brown sugar
+ 300ml double cream
+ 2 tbsp caster sugar
+ 2 egg whites

What you do

Put the greengages in a saucepan with the brown sugar and 250 ml of water. Bring it to the boil, put the lid on and turn down to a simmer for fifteen minutes by which time the greengages should be soft. Push the greengage mixture through a stout sieve and into a bowl trying to leave just the stones and the skins behind. Put the mixture back in the saucepan and reduce by a third to concentrate it. Test for sweetness and add either sugar or lemon juice according to taste. Put in the fridge to cool.

Meanwhile whisk the egg whites in a bowl until they are stiff. Raymond Blanc's trick of adding a small amount of lemon juice helps the process. Then put the double cream in a separate bowl, add the caster sugar and whip till the cream forms peaks.

Gently fold the egg whites into the cream and then carefully stir in the greengage mixture. Don't stir too much as it will make it less airy. Divide among four ramekins or wine glasses. I usually plop a couple of raspberries on top of each because it looks nice. Put back in the fridge and serve cold.

PIPPING COX

I'm not a pudding person. After I've eaten two good courses I don't want something sweet, sticky and heavy to clog my palate. Puddings, like aperitifs, should leave your palate feeling clean and refreshed. A good sorbet can do that but sticky toffee pudding, cheesecake, or baked Alaska can't.

The suggestion below is ridiculously simple. It costs nothing and takes less than two minutes to make. Don't be ashamed to try it, particularly around Christmas when your stomach is under siege from carbohydrates.

I like it so much I actually smile after eating it.

Ingredients for one

+ 1 Cox's Orange Pippin, or any other good apple like a russet. It must be crisp, sweet and sharp. Cox's have the perfect balance of sharpness, flavour and sweetness. Under no circumstances use anything grown in France where they have the worst apples in the world. Have you ever tried a French Golden Delicious?

+ 1 juicy lemon

+ 1 tsp sugar

What you do

Slice the unpeeled apple vertically into very thin circular or part-circular slices, discarding the core when you have finished. A normal-sized apple should give you about fifteen thin slices. Spread these out on a plate and squeeze the juice of a good lemon over them. Sprinkle a little sugar over the slices. Mix them up with a fork and arrange tidily on the plate.

Eat with a small fork. Smile.

NO BREAD
SUMMER
PUDDING

I love Summer Pudding. Everyone loves Summer Pudding. The tartness of the fruits, the fragrance of the juice, the richness of the cream, the feeling of summer… but, but, what does the bread contribute? Do you ever hear anyone say, "I love the soggy white bread soaking up the juice from the berries."?

My summer pudding is every bit as summery as the conventional one but has no bread and no sugar. And it has alcohol. This is a grown-up summer pudding and I know no finer dessert. It can also be made in less than five minutes. It needs no cooking.

A note on the fruit. Raspberries must be the heart of summer pudding. Redcurrants to add some tang. I avoid blackcurrants as being too sharp and we get blackcurrant in the *crème de cassis*, see later. Blackberries are good if you have picked them yourself in a hedgerow but supermarket blackberries look good but are always sharp and unripe. Sometimes I add blueberries for background and sometimes I think, "Nah, too bland," and leave them out. Blueberries are after all a recent American import. Do they deserve a place in the quintessential English pudding? Hmmm. As for strawberries. No thanks. Most bought strawberries are red on the outside and unripe white inside. If you grow your own and have truly ripe strawberries, just eat them by themselves with some cream. Their special flavour will be lost in this pudding.

The alcohol is a key to this pudding. If you don't drink alcohol, please find another dessert. Most important is the crème de cassis, blackcurrant liqueur. You don't need another alcohol but I like a dash of triple sec (Cointreau), and then I round it out with elderflower cordial for extra fragrance. With these additions to give sweetness, the traditional sugar is not needed.

Ingredients for four

+ 350g raspberries
+ 100g redcurrants (frozen is fine)
+ 100g blueberries (optional)
+ 100g wild blackberries (optional)
+ 150ml crème de cassis blackcurrant liqueur (I like Briottet)
+ 50ml triple sec or Cointreau (optional)
+ 50ml elderflower cordial (optional)
+ Cream or crème fraiche

What you do

Put all the fruit in a bowl. Add the liqueurs and cordial. Stir. Put in the fridge and serve cold with dollops of crème fraiche or cream. Make sure when people help themselves that they scoop up plenty of the rich juice from the bottom of the bowl.

PARMESAN, PEARS AND HONEY

This may be my favourite dessert, but, first, a warning. Like all very simple things, you have to use the finest ingredients. The parmesan must be aged and crumbly. The pears must be just ripe, neither hard nor soft, and getting a ripe pear in England is a challenge, but most important is the honey. You have to make this with Seggiano chestnut honey. You probably already know Seggiano. They make first quality Italian ingredients and have a whole range of delectable raw honeys. There is however nothing to match their chestnut honey. It is thick, scented, and rich, with a slightly bitter aftertaste. I've tried many other chestnut honeys. Some come close but none is the real thing set alongside Seggiano. You can find it in many Italian delis or on-line.

Ingredients for four

+ 4 perfectly ripe pears
+ 200g finest parmesan
+ 4 tbsp Seggiano chestnut honey

What you do

First peel the pears. Stand each peeled pear in the middle of an elegant dessert plate. Simplicity needs elegance. With the end of a stout knife chunk off crumbly chunks of parmesan, each the size of a sugar lump or a bit bigger. Arrange these in a loose circle around the pear. Get a big tablespoon of honey and drizzle it over the parmesan chunks. Serve with a knife and fork so you can slice the pear and mix it with the honey and cheese. Stand back for stunned applause. This is so good that if you can't find a pear, make it with just crumbled parmesan and drizzled Seggiano honey…

Accompaniments

On the whole good ingredients, well-cooked, don't need things to tart them up. Tomato ketchup, for instance is a good way of adding taste to boring or bland things. You wouldn't add ketchup to a perfectly grilled lamb chop or steamed sea bass. However, I have three accompaniments on the following pages that go with the very simplest and finest food; roast chicken, perfect lamb, and a green salad, and that make all three of those wonderful dishes kick up their heels and dance

DESMOND'S BREAD SAUCE

Bread sauce is a love-it or hate-it thing. Hate-its, turn the page now, I'm not talking to you, but your roast chicken and your Christmas turkey won't be half as good as mine, nestled under their thick slather of bread sauce.

Bread sauce is as mediaeval as the Black Prince. In the way-back-when before the Columbian Exchange of the 16th century whereby the newly discovered Americas gave us potatoes and syphilis while we gave them chickens and measles, carbs were hard to find in an English kitchen as we had no spuds and the Italians hadn't told us about spaghetti and pizza. Bread was the chief source of carbs and we used it to thicken gravies, to encase juicy berries (summer pudding), as dug-out trenchers to eat off, and for mopping up the left-overs. Left-over bread we mixed with milk and a few spices newly arrived from the East and, voila, bread sauce.

It's very simple to make but, please, ignore your usual Food God's recipe and make mine instead. It's better for two reasons. I don't use breadcrumbs because breadcrumbs give you a slimy bread sauce. I like my bread sauce as I like my mashed potatoes with enough body to fight back and maybe the odd lump. And they put an onion in the sauce, studded with cloves, but then they take it out. Huh? What's not to like about onion in your bread sauce?

I call my sauce after my near neighbour in Norfolk, Desmond MacCarthy of Wiveton Hall. Desmond is as mediaeval as the Black Prince. I once watched him cook dinner for ten people. Recently shot and semi-plucked game birds, wild ducks, partridge, pheasant, and maybe a pigeon or two were popped into the oven while he made the bread sauce. I don't know what his recipe was but I watched in fascination as he tore up chunks of stale bread and tossed them into the milk, just as a medieval housewife would have done, not a breadcrumb to be seen. And that is what I have done ever since which is I why I christened this after him.

Those of you who watch television may know Desmond. He has been the star of two BBC2 four-part documentary series in 2016 and 2017 entirely about his cunning schemes to keep his lunatic house, Wiveton Hall, and its small surrounding farm solvent and self-sustaining. The series was called "Normal for Norfolk". Desmond is now a star. He is easily recognisable from his majestic eyebrows, so large and bushy that birds are suspected to nest in them.

Ingredients for enough bread sauce to accompany a small turkey

+ 1l full cream milk

+ Four or five slices of stale good bread (not supermarket sliced bread)

+ 1 large onion

+ 150g butter

+ Splodge of double cream

+ Cloves

+ 1 tsp of grated nutmeg

+ 1 tsp of dried thyme (optional)

What you do

Put the milk on to warm and leave it at a simmer. Cut the onion in half. Stud one half with ten or so cloves and slice the other half very finely. Put all the onion, studded and sliced, in the milk and leave to simmer.

After fifteen minutes take out the clove-studded half and discard. Take most of the crust off the bread although leaving a bit on will give the sauce some extra body. Tear four slices into chunks and add to the milk while stirring. Add the nutmeg and thyme. Add lots of salt and pepper. Simmer gently for twenty minutes giving the odd stir. The mixture should now be thick enough so that a splodge put on a plate will stay the same shape but not thick enough to be gummy. Adjust the texture by adding more bread if too runny or more milk if too gummy. Simmer a bit more to allow that to assimilate. Just before serving add the butter and cream. Stir them in well over a low heat, decant into a bowl and serve. By the way, this is not a slimmer's sauce. If you want to reduce the calories a bit, leave out the cream but don't leave out the butter.

MINT
RELISH

This goes well with any lamb dish
but is designed to be the main
accompaniment to my favourite dish,
Boiled Sheep Bits (p.94). Make lots of it
and splosh several large spoonfuls on
the side of everyone's plates, not the
usual relish-like dab.

Ingredients for six

+ 6 handfuls of mint
+ 1 handful finely-chopped spring onions
+ 1 tsp ground ginger or two tsps chopped fresh
  ginger
+ 400ml Greek yoghurt
+ 1 tbsp honey
+ Juice of 1 lime
+ 1 tsp chilli flakes

What you do

Destalk mint and chop finely. Put in a bowl
with the chopped spring onions and the other
ingredients. Mix well with a spoon. Taste and
maybe add some salt. Shouldn't need pepper.

MUSTARD VINAIGRETTE

There must be a million different ways to dress a salad. Every newspaper cookery column has to add its own tweak. For me a vinaigrette is like a martini. The more you mess with the basic recipe, the worse it gets. The classic vinaigrette, or "French dressing" as it used to be called, has just three ingredients with one optional extra. The three ingredients are Dijon mustard, oil, and vinegar. The optional extra is a pinch of something to add sweetness, usually sugar. What a martini is to cocktails, this vinaigrette is to dressings. You can't improve on it. Don't mess with it.

Mustard vinaigrette keeps for a long time. You don't need to refrigerate it because that will make the oil go sludgy. I always make a big jar and keep it on the kitchen counter.

Ingredients for a 500ml jar

+ 300ml good olive oil (if you prefer a lighter dressing you can use half olive oil and half of a lighter vegetable oil, like sunflower)

+ 100ml white wine or cider vinegar

+ 1½ tbsp Dijon mustard

+ 1 tbsp honey

What you do

Put the honey and mustard in the jar, followed by the oil and vinegar. Put the lid on the jar tightly and shake vigorously.

How to use it

This works brilliantly on any green salad. I sometimes add chopped walnuts to the salad before sprinkling on the vinaigrette. Use it sparingly. A tablespoon is enough for a salad for two people. Too much dressing will give you soggy salads. Always put it on at the last minute before serving to keep the salad crisp. It works perfectly with any kind of raw vegetables from sliced tomatoes to halved avocadoes.

Drinks

You may have noticed that this is not a book for teetotallers. A stream of alcohol runs through my recipes and all the better they are for alcohol's way of giving richness, flavour, and depth to a dish. There are times though when you just need a drink, alcohol and no food. You already have your favourite cocktail recipes so I won't repeat them here. Mine is a vodka martini, on the rocks with a twist of lemon, the perfect cocktail, simplicity itself with just two ingredients. But you don't need me to tell you how to make it. You already have your own unbeatable recipe.

The recipes on the following pages are ones I largely made up myself. I have a reputation for giving good parties. I would like to take the credit for that but I can't. My secret is giving people a cocktail when they arrive. "Ooo, I hope this isn't too strong?" "Strong? Not at all. Basically just fruit juice." And indeed most of my cocktails taste as if they are innocuous but that is because the combination of citrus and strong spirits is a deceptive one. The citrus comes to the fore and the spirits lurk behind the sofa with a club.

As you will see I have a particular love for rum, bottled sunshine. There are a million rum cocktails and you know many of them, the mojito, the daiquiri and the punches but on the following pages you will find one that is my favourite, the Gay Piranha. It is made from Brazilian rum, *rhum agricole*, or cachaça as it is called in Brazil. It tastes as gentle and harmless as a Caribbean breeze. Give your guests a couple of Gay Piranhas and they will be swinging from the chandeliers.

GREENGAGE VODKA

The Alsatians do exquisite fruit brandies, their eaux de vie, Mirabelle, Kirsch, Poire Williams and many others. To make these they take huge quantities of fruit, as much as fifteen kilos of pears to make one bottle of Poire, ferment it for weeks and then distil the resulting liquor to produce something ethereal when you drink it ice-cold after a good dinner.

In England we are less subtle. We take the fruit and macerate it in gin, vodka or any other spirit for a period before straining it to produce, for instance, Sloe Gin. I have never been a big admirer of these English home brews so I set to making a greengage vodka with only moderate enthusiasm. The results blew me away. Do try it. It could not be simpler to make. It's a wonderful aperitif with a couple of lumps of ice, or, chilled in the freezer, a stunning after-dinner drink. Here's what I did.

Ingredients for one-litre bottle

+ 1kg ripe greengages

+ 125g caster sugar

+ 750ml vodka

What you do

Make sure the greengages are clean. (Wash them if you're a hygiene person but not too much as you will wash away the natural yeasts if you do.) Cut each one into two or three pieces but don't bother to remove the stones. Put the cut greengages in a big Kilner or Mason jar. Add the sugar and vodka, close the lid and give the jar a good shake.

Leave the jar in a cool, dark place for a week by which time the liquor will have gone a browny-gold.

Strain the jar's contents through muslin into a bowl. Squeeze the muslin to make sure you get all the liquid out. Discard the pulp and stones. Pour the greengage vodka through a funnel into a clean glass bottle. I use the bottle that the vodka came from.

Chill and drink, preferably after dinner. It is slightly sweet. Delicious.

PINK PANTHER

From time to time a booze-free week is a good idea. Regrettable but true. Foregoing wine with dinner is hard because there are no good wine substitutes. Apple juice? I think not. No-alcohol wine? I think definitely not. The other difficult time is cocktail time. It's an hour before dinner. You have friends around. They are drinking delicious cocktails.

You would like to be drinking a delicious cocktail but it's a no-booze day. Here's when I make a Pink Panther. I won't say it's as good as a vodka martini because nothing is that good but it's a fine drink. You can take it to the table with you and drink it with dinner too. I don't know a better, or easier to make, non-alcoholic drink. It has the added virtue of being, unlike many non-alcoholic drinks, all but calorie-free. Try it. You'll enjoy it. You may even forget you're not drinking alcohol.

Ingredients for one drink

+ Good sparkling water (I like San Pellegrino)
+ Angostura bitters
+ 1 lime wedge

What you do

Fill an old-fashioned glass or half-tumbler one-third full with ice. Add half a dozen shakes of Angostura. Fill up with San Pellegrino. Squeeze the lime quarter over the drink and drop it in. Drink. Good, isn't it?

RUM: THE GAY PIRANHA AND LE TI' PUNCH

Who doesn't like a lime, the essence of freshness and zing, its sharpness hiding an inner sweetness. The mixture of lime, rum and ice is sublime. It forms the base of so many of the world's great cocktails, the daiquiri, mojito, and caipirinha being the holy trinity of rum cocktails.

Rum divides into three distinct types. Most rums are made not from distilling sugar-cane juice but from distilling molasses, a sugar by-product. In the English and Spanish-speaking islands all rum is made from molasses. Bacardi, Mount Gay, Havana Club, Captain Morgan and Appleton's all start as molasses. The French-speaking islands are different. Most of their rum is distilled directly from sugar-cane spirit. This is called ç. The best-known producers are in Martinique and Guadeloupe although both Haiti and Mauritius also produce fine *rhums agricoles* with many people, including me, feeling that Haiti's Barbancourt is the best of all. Other great *rhums agricoles* are St James, Depaz, J.M., and Clément. The third kind of rum is produced in Brazil and only in Brazil. It is called cachaça. Cachaça is a *rhum agricole*, produced just like the Martinique *agricoles* directly from cane spirit distilled in copper pot stills. The best cachaças are often aged in barrels made of exotic Brazilian hardwoods, each one imparting a different flavour and a golden or yellow colour to the cachaça.

The molasses-based rums tend to be sweeter, rounder, and more mellow in taste. They can be coloured with caramel to darken them and even if they're not, they still often have a caramelly taste. They go well in cocktails, particularly punches where they are mixed with fruit juice.

The *rhums agricoles* and cachaças are drier, more fragrant, often with a wild, grassy scent, and they are usually white and they are usually high in alcohol. If the molasses rums are good for fruit punches, the agricoles and cachaças are best for the simple but unbeatable lime and rum cocktails. If the molasses rums are bourbon, the agricoles are single-malt Scotch.

You can look up recipes easily enough for rum punches and the normal rum cocktails like mojitos (for which I would use an agricole) but below are two of my favourite rum and lime, or rather, rhum and lime, cocktails with which you may be less familiar.

First is the Gay Piranha, This is my version of the caipirinha. The caipirinha, all but unknown outside Brazil ten years ago, is taking the world by storm. I suspect that cachaça will replace tequila as the world's next spirit craze. At present huge quantities of cachaça are produced but almost 99% stays in Brazil. You make a caipirinha with lime, brown sugar, ice and cachaça and wonderfully good it is. My Gay Piranha version substitutes triple sec (e.g. Cointreau) for the sugar. Triple sec is a terrific cocktail mixer, think sidecars, margaritas, and white ladies. It adds smoothness and suavity to a drink. And why is this called a Gay Piranha? Several years ago, when I began making it, an ethereal young woman who couldn't pronounce caipirinha, said to me, "Milo, what's that great cocktail you do? It's called something like a gay piranha." And so it has stayed.

What the martini is to Manhattan, the ti' Punch is to Martinique. It is as simple as a martini and one of the best cocktails, almost unknown outside the French Caribbean. Btw, ti' is French Creole for petit.

Ingredients for one Gay Piranha

+ ½ lime cut into small pieces
+ 50ml cachaça
+ 25ml triple sec or Cointreau
+ Small-cube or crushed ice

What you do

Put the cut-up lime pieces in an old-fashioned glass or half-tumbler. Squash them with a muddler or other blunt object to release the juice. Fill the glass with small-cube or crushed ice. Add the triple sec and cachaça. Cover the top of the glass with your left hand, slide a teaspoon between your thumb and index-finger and jiggle the teaspoon vigorously for a few seconds to blend everything together. Taste and adjust for sweetness with a dash more triple sec or lime juice.

This is my favourite cocktail. When you have had a few you will realise why it reminds me of a terrible old joke – What do a caipirinha and a woman's breasts have in common? One is not enough, but three is too many.

Ingredients for one ti' Punch

+ ½ lime
+ 25-50ml *rhum agricole* (amount depending on size of your glass)
+ 1 tsp sugar or sugar syrup (I use triple sec instead)
+ 1 big lump of ice or two smaller ones

What you do

Take a small glass, preferably halfway between a shot glass and a half-tumbler. Ideally it should be narrow, about the diameter of a lime. Squeeze the juice out of the half-lime into the glass and drop the squeezed lime into the glass. Add sugar, stir, and then the ice. Pour the *rhum* over the ice and give it another good stir.

Once again, I substitute triple sec for the sugar but either is good. The good ol' boys in Martinique don't use ice. When they order a ti' Punch in a bar, the bartender pushes them over a lime, a knife, a bottle of *rhum* and some sugar. They mix their own.

SANGRIA PARALITICO

Several years ago I had to go to a business meeting with five high-powered Americans in Madrid. It was to be in the Madrid Ritz, one of the world's most stylish hotels. I decided to go there on my motorbike, taking three days to get there through France and over the Pyrenees, returning on the ferry from Bilbao. A lovely trip.

I arrived just after noon, dirty and travel-stained from the road. An immaculate doorman unloaded my panniers and took my bike off for a good cleaning. I checked in, showered, put on crisp, clean clothes, and looked at my watch. It was two in the afternoon. The Americans would not be arriving till five. I sauntered down to the Ritz's elegant garden, parked myself in the shade, opened my book and, it being a hot day, ordered an inoffensive jug of sangria. At four I ordered a second jug. It was cool and refreshing, not too much of the fruit salad that tourist restaurants put in sangria.

The afternoon drifted by, the book was excellent, and at 5.30 pm there was a cry from arriving Americans, "Hey, Miles, buddy, how you doing?"

I jumped to my feet to greet them and suddenly realised that my legs were buckling at the knees. I was going down, Titanic-style. I was literally legless. I grasped my chair and sat down quickly before I did a face-plant across the Ritz lawn.

"Hi, guys, hi…" I stammered out. "Whoops, just feeling a bit faint. Hot day. Bit faint. I'll catch you at dinner."

Somehow, after a fifteen-minute pause and a glass or two of water, I managed to make it up to my room, have a long cold shower, and join the Americans for dinner.

Two months later I was back in England and had a group of people who didn't know each other coming to an alfresco lunch. What could I give them to get things going? I emailed the Ritz Madrid, for the attention of the Head Barman. How did he make his sangria? The next day an email in Spanish came back with the recipe, *"Una botella de Rioja, una copa de coñac…"* You may think sangria a debased drink, cheap wine, fruit salad, cheap fizz… That's what it usually is. But not at the Madrid Ritz. Here's the English translation of his recipe.

Ingredients for a jug enough for six, four if you're thirsty

+ Lots of ice

+ 1 bottle (750ml) decent red Rioja or similar, chilled

+ 1 glass (250ml) Spanish brandy

+ 1 glass (250ml) Cointreau or triple sec

+ 1 orange, cut into chunks, sprinkled with a little cinnamon

+ 1 glass (250ml) dry ginger ale or lemonade (optional)

What you do

Pour the wine, brandy, and Cointreau into the jug over the ice. Add the orange chunks giving them enough of a squeeze to release some juice, top up with ginger ale, stir and serve in long glasses. After three glasses don't attempt to stand up.

CORFU COOLER

I discovered this drink in Corfu when I was in my twenties and have used it as a go-to hot weather drink ever since. It is cheap, it is easy to make, it uses simple local ingredients, and it has enough alcohol to give it taste but not enough to give you a fuzzy head on a hot afternoon. It is first cousin to an Americano and to a spritzer. The base is vermouth. When people think of vermouth they think of Martini, Cinzano, and the great French white vermouths such as Noilly Prat. Those are excellent. Vermouth is wine that has been mixed with herbs, roots and barks, and had a shot of alcohol added to it. The name comes from Wermut, the German word for wormwood, an ingredient in some vermouths.

The Mediterranean is full of wonderful local vermouths, locally made, and offered at a very cheap price. For this drink, seek one of those out rather than using Martini or Cinzano. You can make it with red vermouth or white. The white is more refreshing, the red has more taste.

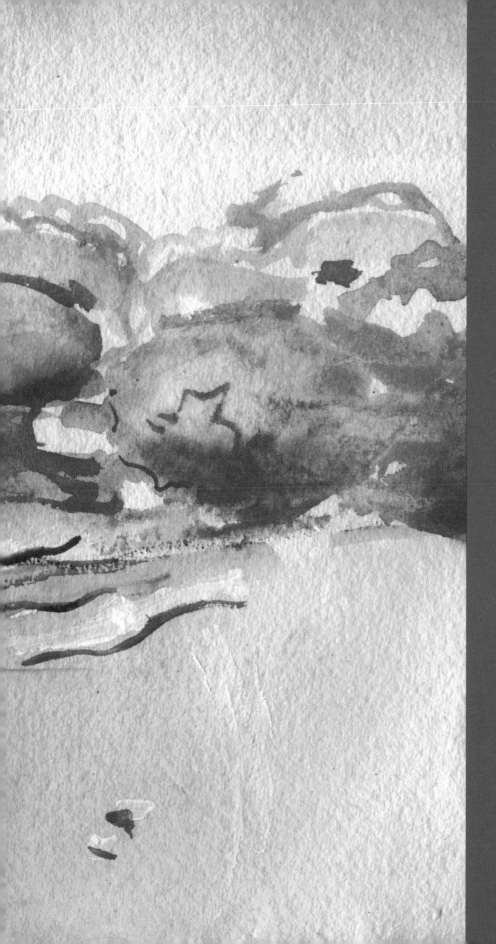

Ingredients for one Corfu Cooler

+ Vermouth
+ Soda water
+ Ice
+ ½ orange slice

What you do

Take a tall highball glass. Fill it a third full of ice. Pour the vermouth over the ice till the glass is half full. Top up with soda and drop in the orange slice with a squeeze.

Man Learns to Drink

When I was in my twenties, wine was an unknown world asking to be explored. I didn't know my Beaujolais from my Burgundy. Like so many of the most rewarding things the more you got to know about it the more interesting it became. My earliest wine education was free. In the late 1960s I was working at one of the great English merchant banks. We were expected to have private incomes (I didn't). This was before the great English merchant banks began calling themselves investment banks and sold their birthrights to foreign firms. Schroders, the firm I worked at, does exist today but solely as a specialist money management firm, the main investment bank part of it having been flogged off to Citibank.

In the late 1960s, Christie's the auctioneers, were rebuilding a wine auction business, wine auctions having stopped during the war. The day before their auctions one or sometimes two or three bottles of every case of wine that was going to be offered for sale the next day was opened and available for tasting. I would pop on to the tube and head off to King Street in St James's, usually with "Slim" Fraser, a giant Australian who was also working at Schroders. There, through a discreet entrance next to Christie's headquarters, was the wine auction room. Buying a catalogue at the door gave you free access to a room where, arrayed on tables spread with white cloths, were a hundred or more different wines. If you got there late the samples of the more precious ones would have been finished. Slim and I got there early.

You could taste wines which if they came up for sale today would go for thousands of pounds a bottle: 1945 Mouton Rothschild, 1949 Romanée-Conti, or even the legendary 1961 Lafite although then at such a young age it was hardly drinkable. It wasn't just the clarets and the great Burgundies. There were Hermitage and Côte Rôtie from the Rhône, German Rieslings with their unique combination of honey and steel, and of course port including some of the legendary 1948s.

The other tasters were chiefly from the trade and went methodically round the tables, jotting in their notebooks and never swallowing the wines, simply rolling them round their palates, inhaling through the mouth to put oxygen over them, chewing a couple of times to feel the flavour, and then spitting into the funnels of the spittoons which were stationed on all the tables. Not us. We had gone through the catalogue on the tube noting the outstanding wines, the ones which were likely to be finished early, and we were not intending to waste time tasting a cru bourgeois while there were bottles of Latour 1945 and Fonseca 1948 with something in them still to drink.

Nor did we spit; we swallowed. We arrived at 12.15pm, quarter of an hour after the doors opened. We left at 1.30pm, having told the people on our desk at Schroders that we might be a little late back as we had to go to an important meeting in the West End. At around 2.00pm we staggered back into Schroders, having swallowed gulps of thirty or forty of the world's finest wines.

The latter half of those wine-tasting afternoons were muddled. I usually had to retreat to the Schroders men's room and spend much of the rest of the afternoon with my head down the loo. My hope was that the Earl of Airlie, my Schroders boss, and later the Queen's Lord Chamberlain, didn't come into the men's room and hear one of his junior analysts throwing up.

But I did learn a lot about wine.

Some Tips on Wine

1 Drink as much as you can. The only way to learn about wine is to drink it. Reading about "wine with the scent of evening violets and notes of cedar", will only baffle you as much as it does me. I suspect wine writers are pulling our legs when they write things like that. The more wine you drink the more interesting it becomes and the better you can tell what makes wine taste good to you.

2 Trust your own palate. The same wine tastes different to different people. Just as some people like chocolate and others like Marmite, some people's palates are drawn to dry, flinty wines while others like their wine full-bodied and rich.

3 Don't pay much attention to wine writers. Their palates have been trained. That took years. Consequently they will recognise things in the wine you can't. Most of them also have to keep an eye on the advertisers. You don't.

4 Wine hates being moved around. It's madness to pick up a bottle in a shop, jolt and jiggle it home, or, even worse, to a friend's house, and then drink it. The jiggling will make it taste harsh and sharp. Always try to give a bottle of wine a few days' rest before you open it. When a friend coming to dinner is kind enough to bring you a nice bottle, say, "Thankyou, this looks delicious. I'll put it somewhere cool to rest for a few days and look forward to drinking it then."

5 Forty years ago it was difficult to find good wine. Now, thanks to modern agriculture and wine-making techniques, it is difficult to find bad wine, and good wines can often be found at a very reasonable price.

6 Forty years ago, France and Italy dominated both cooking and wine-making. French and Italian wines, port, and, to a lesser extent, German Rieslings, were the only wines people took seriously. Spanish wine then tasted of dirty barrels, American wine was coarse, Australian wine was coarser, Eastern European and Greek wines were a taste hazard, Chile and Argentina were clumsy infants, and everywhere else was a joke. Today France and Italy have both upped their game, particularly in the non-classic areas, like Gascony and Puglia, but meanwhile the rest of the world has been transformed. Rioja has lost the taste of dirty barrels and is now a vanilla-scented marvel, Greek assyrtiko, Argentinian malbec, Chilean merlot, Tasmanian champagne, Margaret River cabernet, Sicilian vermentino, Portuguese verdelho and touriga nacional, Californian zinfandel and so many others are wines whose freshness and depth of flavour can blow your socks off. Who can say if they are better or worse than a classic Bordeaux or super-Tuscan? It's like trying to compare steak with cauliflower.

7 When in doubt go for wine from somewhere sunny. You can't make good wine without sunshine. When they get the sunshine, climatically challenged areas like Burgundy and Champagne, can turn out extraordinary wines but when they don't their wines, particularly the ones you can afford, will be sharp in Burgundy and green and stalky in Champagne. On the other hand, a wine from the southern Rhône, probably my favourite wine area in the world, is always going to be full of sunshine.

8 Everyone likes eating in ethnic restaurants but what to drink with Chinese, Indian or Thai if you don't go for beer? Ethnic restaurants often have dodgy wine lists foisted on them by cynical merchants off-loading second-rate French and Italian wines with posh-sounding names on them. Hello Mouton Cadet. The French and Italians can, even today, make some really bad wines, many of which find their way to the wine lists of Thai, Chinese and Indian restaurants. On the other hand, the Chileans never make a bad wine. Chile may not make the best wines in the world but its combination of climate and technology means they are always a pleasure to drink. Eat Chinese, drink Chilean is a good motto.

9 When you are travelling it's nice to taste the local wines, particularly now that so many places are turning out good wine. There is one unbreakable rule. Never buy a wine produced in the tropics. Grapes need a dormant season to produce drinkable wine. There are no seasons in the tropics. People have tried starving tropical vines of water for part of the year to simulate a dormant season but it doesn't work. It's so easy to buy good wines these days, the majority produced in places with a Mediterranean climate, that a spirit of perversity makes me seek out really bad wines on my travels, just for fun. The winners, the world's worst wines; a Kenyan Lake Naivasha red, a Bolivian white, a Vietnamese Central Highlands Chablis, an Ethiopian burgundy, and a Madagascan rosé, were all from the tropics.

10 I travel a lot. What a joy it is to be somewhere you don't associate with wine and get a wonderful surprise. That has happened to me in northern Mexico, Japan (a merlot), Syria, all through the Balkans, Israel, Tunisia, and Turkey.

11 There are so many brilliant wines these days that it's hard to go wrong. I give you a personal list below of wines and wine types that I love. These are not always obvious wine choices. I love Bordeaux and Burgundy and some of the great Italian wines but you don't need me to give you advice on those.

Wines I love

Southern Rhônes

Sunshine in a bottle. This is a land of amazing red wines but don't ignore the whites, equally redolent of sunshine and spice. It's difficult to go wrong with a basic Côtes du Rhône, but if you want to trade up look for Gigondas, Seguret, Rasteau, Vacqueyras and Ventoux. King of the Southern Rhônes (perhaps Pope is more appropriate) is Châteauneuf-du-Pape, my favourite wine, but it is expensive. Just across the river is Lirac, its twin area many years ago considered superior to Châteauneuf. The wines are similar but at half the price. Get some.

Gascony

Nowhere in France has seen a bigger improvement in wine-making in the last fifty years than Gascony, the South West. The area used to make thin, cheap supermarket wines, bulked out with strong wine imported from Algeria until the EU discouraged the import of Algerian wine. The old vineyards of the South West were grubbed up and better varieties planted. Go and hunt for some. Names to look for are Corbières, Cahors, the original malbec, Saint-Mont, Irouléguy, Madiran and many others. These wines have great depth, wines to put hair on your chest.

Cassis and Bandol

Two small fishing towns east of Marseilles, both producing wines of giant flavour heady with spice.

Alsace.

France's great "secret". The French love their Alsatian wines, so much so that only a small proportion is exported. These are the great white wines, so elegant in their tall, green bottles, of the brasseries. Riesling is the "serious" Alsatian wine. Some Rieslings are lovely although they can be too austere and minerally for me. I prefer the luscious Pinot Gris, the bewitching Gewürztraminers, and the plainer Pinot Blancs and Sylvaners. My favourite though is an unusual wine, a dry Alsatian Muscat. Muscat, with its rich sweetness usually makes sweet, grapey wines. In Alsace they make a dry Muscat which keeps the fragrance but loses most of the sweetness. Alsatian wines can be expensive. I buy mine from the Wine Society who have an excellent selection, including a delicious dry Muscat, at very reasonable prices.

Tasmanian champagne.

I motorbiked around Tasmania a few years ago and discovered these. They are not easy to find in England but Jansz is now available. It's about half the price of an equivalent French champagne.

Tawny Port.

No-one drinks port these days. That is a mistake. Vintage port is a wonderful drink but it is expensive and decanting it is a faff. Tawny port, matured in the barrel rather than the bottle, is lighter both in colour and taste. It doesn't need decanting. It's less than half the price of vintage. Taylor's and Graham's, among others, make wonderful tawnies. The 10-year olds are good, the 20-year olds sublime.

Harvey's Bristol Cream sherry.

Please, don't go all snobby on me. Go out and buy a bottle for just over a tenner, put it in the fridge, and have a glass after dinner. A ridiculously under-rated wine.

Index

Vodka Martini Press
vodkamartinipress.com

First published in Great Britain 2021
by Vodka Martini Press

Design by Emma Charleston
emmacharleston.co.uk

ISBN: 978-1-7398372-0-4

Printed and bound in the UK by Gemini Print Group
gemini-print.co.uk